The Ultimate Query Letter Tool Kit

by

Writer's Relief, Inc.

Helping writers prepare and target their submissions since 1994

The Ultimate Query Letter Tool Kit
Copyright: Writer's Relief, Inc.
Published: September 2020
ISBN: 978-0-9963228-5-0
Publisher: Writer's Relief, Inc.

ALL RIGHTS RESERVED. No part of this manual may be reproduced or transmitted for resale or use by any party other than the individual purchaser, who is the sole authorized user of this information. Purchaser is authorized to use any of the information in this publication for his or her own use ONLY. All other reproduction or transmission, in any form or by any means, electronic or mechanical, including photocopying, recording, or by any information storage or retrieval system, is prohibited without express written permission from Writer's Relief, Inc.

LEGAL NOTICES: While all attempts have been made to provide effective, verifiable information in this manual, neither the author nor publisher assumes any responsibility for errors, inaccuracies, or omissions. Any slights of people or organizations are unintentional. If advice concerning tax, legal, compliance, or related matters is needed, the services of a qualified professional should be sought. This manual is not a source of legal, regulatory compliance, or accounting information, and it should not be regarded as such. This publication is designed to provide accurate and authoritative information in regard to the subject matter covered. It is sold with the understanding that the publisher is not engaged in rendering legal, accounting, or other professional service. If legal advice or other expert assistance is required, the services of a competent professional should be sought. Due to the nature of publishing and varying rules regulating related activities in many fields, licensee and/or purchaser must accept full responsibility for determining the legality and/or ethical character of any and all business and publishing transactions and/or practices adopted and enacted in his or her particular field and geographic location, whether or not those transactions and/or practices are suggested, either directly or indirectly, in this manual. As with any business and publishing advice, the reader is strongly encouraged to seek professional counsel before taking action. NOTE: No guarantees of income or profits are intended or promised in this publication. Many variables affect individual results. Your results may vary. Writer's Relief, Inc. has no control over what you may do or not do with the information contained in this publication and therefore cannot accept responsibility for your results. You are the only one who can initiate the proper action in order to succeed in publishing your work.

Published by: Writer's Relief, Inc., Rehoboth Beach, DE 19971

© Writer's Relief, Inc., 2020

Table Of Contents

Introduction 1

Part One: Welcome To The Building Blocks Of Query Letters
What's The Difference Between A Cover Letter And A Query Letter? 7
Publishing Industry Submissions: Basic Vocabulary 9
Basic Query Letter Submission Format 12

Part Two: Blueprint For Success
6 Strategies To Implement Before You Start 16
Approach Your Query Letter With The Right Mindset 20
Know Thy Book: Is It Fiction? Nonfiction? Or Something Else? 22
Novels: The Right Genre, Subgenre, Word Count 23
Memoir: The 4 Pre-Query Factors That Will Influence Your Success 29
Nonfiction Query Letters: How To Prepare Before You Query 31
7 Easy Ways To Build Your Reputation For Your Book Query 34

Part Three: The Nuts And Bolts Of Your Novel And Memoir Query Letter
The 5 Common Elements Of Novel And Memoir Query Letters:
    Element #1: Greetings And Salutations 37
    Element #2: Introduce Your Book The Right Way 38
        Query Chestnuts: Opening Lines That Rarely Work 42
        Comparing Your Book To Similar Titles 43
    Element #3: The Book Blurb For Your Novel Or Memoir 46
        Query Letter Book Summary Template 47
        A Useful Structure For Summarizing Your Book 49
        Alternative Book Blurbs 52
        Choose The Right Point Of View For Your Query 55
        Point Of View: Advanced Techniques For Storytellers 56
        The Most Common POV Mistakes In Query Letters 59
        What Your Book Blurb Must Do 60
        5 Essential Strategies For A More…Compelling Query 62
        6 Sample Query Letters For Novels And Memoirs 63
    Element #4: Your Author Bio: Make A Great Impression! 76
        Your Author Bio Checklist 76
        What To Do If You Have No Publishing Credits 78
        Example Of A Bio For A Writer Who Has No Credits 80
        The Publishing Credits Shuffle 81
        Which Kinds Of Publishing Credits Are Best? 83
        Fake Writing Contests And Your Author Bio 86
        Who's Who: The Truth About Special Directories 88

Adding A Personal Note: Useful Or Useless 90
The Right Way To Use Your Pen Name In Your Letter..........92
Element #5: Knowing How To Say Goodbye 94
TMI: 10 Things NOT To Say In Your Query Letter.................95
Your Query Letter Checklist..97

Part Four: How To Assemble An Attention-Getting Summary For Your Nonfiction Book
The Best Way To Structure Your Self-Help And How-To Summary 99
How To Write A Summary: Biography, History, Popular Science 102
3 Examples Of Awesome Bios For Nonfiction Writers................................105
Strategies For Pitching Your Nonfiction Book...106
A Sample Query Letter For Nonfiction That Worked 108

Part Five: Support Materials
Support Materials For Fiction And Memoir 110
Your Synopsis: Writing It Doesn't Have To Be A Chore............................111
The 5 Most Common Synopsis Mistakes..113
Prepare Your Book's Opening Pages..115
Support Materials For Nonfiction Book Proposals 118

Part Six: Custom Designs For Special Query Letters
Querying With Fictionalized Nonfiction (or Nonfiction-y Fiction)...............122
How And When To Mention Multiple Books (Or A Series) 124
Should You Mention Your Self-Publishing History? 126
How To Write A Query For A Self-Published Book 128
Sample Query Letter For A Previously Self-Published Book.....................130
Should You Mention Others Who Helped You Write Your Book?.............132
How To Write A Query For A Book Previously Represented....................134
How To Write A Query For A Short Story Collection 137
Sample Query (Short Story Collection) 139
Sample Query (Novel-In-Stories) 141
How To Write A Query Letter For An Essay Collection............................143
Sample Query (Memoir) 144
Sending A Revised Book To An Agent Who Has Already Seen It 145
Sample Query For A Revised Manuscript 147

Part Seven: Necessary Repairs: What To Do If Your Query Isn't Working
Not Getting Results? How To Think Like An Agent..................................149
6 Shortcuts Agents Will Use To Immediately Reject You 151
11 Common Query Letter Mistakes..154
6 Sentences That Should Never Appear In Your Query 156

Example Of A Very Bad Query (Just For Fun) 157

Part Eight: Query Letter Checklists
Checklists For Your Query Letter 161

Part Nine: More Sample Query Letters
More Sample Query Letters! Compare And Contrast 165

Bonus Section
What's The Purpose Of A Cover Letter 172
Basic Cover Letter Elements 175
How To Ask A Famous Author For A Quote 176
Sample Letter For Requesting An Endorsement Quote 179
15 Tricks That Will Make Life Easier With A Submission Manager 181
The 7 Signs Of A Healthy Submission Strategy 184
How To Stay Motivated When You Want To Quit 186
If You Are Going To Hire A Submission Service 188
Free Resources On Our Website 191
Final Thoughts 193

Introduction: Who We Are And Why You Should Listen To Us

Writer's Relief is an author's submission service, and we've been helping creative writers make submissions since 1994. We're a highly specialized team of personal assistants who have expert knowledge of the publishing industry.

We help book authors find literary agents.

We help poetry, short story, and essay writers get published in literary journals.

As part of our all-inclusive submission management, we collaborate with clients to write their cover and query letters. Our work is personalized, careful, and precise—we're not a "submission factory" and do not support any kind of submission spam. We love writers, and it's our goal to see our clients get published. That means we take a personal, hands-on approach to helping our clients make submissions. The reason we've been in business for 20+ years is that our strategies are ethical and, most of all, they work.

In the decades since we opened our doors, we've had countless clients connect with literary agencies through strong QUERY letters. And a great many of our clients get published in literary magazines with strong COVER letters.

We've also seen just about every mistake a writer can make in a cover or query letter, and we've heard every misinformed idea that can be picked up at a writing conference. We've helped our clients correctly answer many of the tough questions that can arise when writing cover and query letters, such as:

- How do I write a good blurb/summary for my book? Should it give away the ending?

- How do I handle my pen name in my query letters?

- What if I have no publishing credits to list in my author bio? What should I say?

- Should I mention that my book was originally self-published?

- What are the sentences a writer should never include in a query or cover letter?

Now, after many years of offering our expertise to the writers on our limited and exclusive client list, we're thrilled to be able to pass our expert advice along to you!

What You Will Find In This Book
This is a book for *creative writers*: authors of novels, stories, poems, essays, memoirs, and nonfiction books appropriate for literary agent representation. It's NOT a book for freelance writers who are hoping to pitch nonfiction article ideas in query letters to editors at commercial magazines.

In this book you'll find proven strategies for writing query letters. You'll also find sample query letters, including many real letters from Writer's Relief clients that actually worked. We've specified when an example comes from a client's letter. But all examples in this book are effective teaching tools.

Whatever type of letter you're writing or genre you write in, we strongly recommend that you read the whole book. This book is short, but it's packed with great information—once you've finished reading it, you'll have a new, comprehensive perspective on writing effective letters. Knowledge is never wasted.

What You WON'T Find In This Book
This book focuses on letter writing: the strategies of crafting a persuasive query to send agents. If you're reading this book, you probably already have a pretty good idea *why* you need a query letter.

This book is *not* focused on the larger issues that may arise during the submission process, like what to do when you find yourself in a sticky conversation with an agent as a result of your submission. And this is not a writers' market book: we don't offer lists of markets for your query letter. (Sorry! Personalized, precision targeting is part of what we do for our clients.)

To get a sense of the big picture and the larger mechanisms that are at work—the "world" in which your query letter will operate—please check out the additional titles available on our website:

- ***The Writer's Relief Field Guide To Literary Agents:*** *Find, Entice, Keep, And Manage Your Dream Agent.* This book will teach you all about literary agents—who they are, how to connect with them, and whether you need one. It will also explain how to deal with the many problems that can (and will) arise when you begin querying, such as: how to handle requests for exclusivity; how to follow up; how to know if your second-choice agent is good enough; what to do if your agent isn't paying enough attention to you; and how to resubmit.

- ***Publishing Poetry & Prose In Literary Journals.*** This book will introduce you to the world of literary magazines (which primarily publish poems, short stories, and short nonfiction). It also offers solutions to common problems: how to deal with multiple acceptances; negotiating "handshake" contracts; and interpreting rejection letters. We also lay out a clear plan to help you create an effective, reliable system for making regular submissions.

- ***The Happy Writer:*** *Your Secret Weapon Against Rejection, Dejection, Writer's Block, And The Emotional Pitfalls Of The Writing Life.* This book will help you deal with the doldrums and slumps of being a writer. If you're submitting cover or query letters, you *will* get rejections. *The Happy Writer* explains how that can be a good thing, as long as you know how to turn adversity into the fuel for your success.

- ***The Goal-Oriented Writer:*** *How To Define And Organize Your Writing Goals.* **FREE!** This short workbook will help you to clarify your intentions as a writer and to create a plan for meeting your goals. At the time of this writing, *The Goal-Oriented Writer* is offered free to writers who submit samples to our Review Board in the hopes of becoming a Writer's Relief client. We can't guarantee this offer will still be available when you visit our website, but it's worth taking a look to find out. For more information, please visit www.writersrelief.com/submission-guidelines-for-review-board/.

Trust Your Instincts

We've read and written *thousands* of queries over the last 20-plus years, so we have a perspective that is unequaled in the publishing industry. Our advice is based on what we *know* works.

But if you read enough about the writing community, or if you attend enough conferences, you know that there are conflicting opinions about a lot of the topics we will cover in this book. Everyone has his or her own idea about what's best.

What we offer readers is a perspective that is uniquely pro-writer, and while you may not agree with all of our recommendations, we hope we can offer food for thought. Ultimately, you must make your own way within the publishing industry, using your instincts as your guide. From where we stand, we're glad that there's room for debate about the "best practices" for query letters; it means you as a writer have options.

In this book, we'll teach you our methods. Our system might not work for everyone, but learning what we do will help you determine what is best for you. When we work on a query letter, it's always our clients who make the final decisions. We offer advice, but the final choices are yours.

You will notice a little repetition throughout this book; this is deliberate. We believe that some repetition helps make things stick. But also, when you return to this book later on trying to find that "one thing" you meant to remember or to review a certain topic, you'll have an easier time locating what you're looking for.

We've been working with writers for many years, and it's always a thrill when one of our clients calls us to say, "I got another request from an agent!" Our clients have ranged from career academics, to professional bestselling novelists, to promising but unpublished writers. Some clients have amassed many publications in literary magazines and proceed to release books with great publishers. One client sent us 100 bottles of beer to celebrate his 100th publication... Don't worry! We didn't drink them on the job—or all at once!

We would not mislead our clients and say that getting published is easy and straightforward. Often, the very talents that make a writer good at creating a book or poem can work against him or her when it's time to start working on a query letter (and, to a lesser extent, a cover letter).

If you're interested in knowing how Writer's Relief can help you (we can manage as much or as little of the submission process as you like), just find us online or give us a call. We're easy to get in touch with, and we may be able to help you write your query letter. You'll learn more about us as you read this book, since we will often present our own thoughts and strategies to give you a complete picture of your options.

But of course you do not *need* a Writer's Relief submission strategist writing your query letter or cover letter in order to succeed. If you've got the dedication, talent, time, and ability to put what you learn here into your letter—you'll be fine.

Introduction

If this book helps you get an agent or get published, we would love to hear about it. Please contact us and let us know what you think. With your permission, we might even feature your experience on our blog!

Happy reading!

Ronnie L. Smith

Ronnie L. Smith, President
Writer's Relief, Inc.
(866) 405-3003
www.WritersRelief.com

Part One

Welcome To The Building Blocks Of Query Letters

Vocabulary, Concepts, And Background

What's The Difference Between A Cover Letter And A Query Letter?

Cover letters and query letters are the horses and rhinos of the writing world. Are they genetically related? Yes, but you wouldn't mistake one for the other.

Before we go on, one quick note about terminology: In the world of nonfiction freelance writing, query letters are sent to editors to pitch a news story, commentary, or article. But when we talk about a query letter in the context of the book publishing industry, we're talking about the letter a writer sends to a literary agent in order to try to secure representation.

Let's start by looking at the *raison d'être* of both cover letters and query letters. There's a lot of practical strategy to be gleaned by understanding the purpose and function of each type of letter.

What's The Purpose Of A Query Letter?

A query letter is a cover letter with more bells and whistles. A literary agent isn't going to read your manuscript unless you offer a compelling reason as to why you and your book are the complete package—everything an agent is looking for that projects future success. In the book publishing business, there's money to be made. And that means high competition.

Even though there's no guarantee an agent will read your work, most DO read the many query letters that arrive by the hundreds each month. Some agencies have assistants and interns to identify the most promising queries. Some agents skim. Your query is your one shot to convince an agent to request actual pages of your manuscript.

So, in essence, a query letter is a one-page, summarized introduction that's similar to a cover letter, but the subtext of a query is: *I'm an awesome writer who has a fabulous, unique book that's definitely worth a read.*

These days, the majority of agents request that query letters be sent without any accompanying materials (such as a synopsis or sample pages). After reading your one-page query, the agent will decide if he or she wants to see more materials.

It's a good idea to have your synopsis and sample pages ready *before* you send out your query letter so that you can quickly respond to requests. We can't stress this enough: be prepared! The last thing you want to do if an agent actually requests materials is to keep him or her waiting.

Here's what you should have ready *before* you send out query letters:

For Memoirs And Novels:

Your completed manuscript. Proofread, prepped, and formatted to industry standards. If you don't know about industry standard formatting, contact us through our website and ask for our free formatting guidelines.

Sample pages. The *first* pages of your novel or memoir. Agents usually ask for between twenty-five and one hundred sample pages.

Synopsis. A summary of your book that's between one and three pages long. We'll teach you how to create a well-written synopsis in an upcoming section.

For Nonfiction (excluding memoir):

Book proposal. Your helpful book about dieting, the history of war, or the science of meditation doesn't need to be completed prior to submission. Yes, you read that right. It does not have to be finished before you pitch your idea to agents.

However, you will need a substantial book proposal that includes sample chapters and market analysis, among other things. You'll also need a strong author platform. We'll explain more about this topic in another section.

Publishing Industry Submissions: Basic Vocabulary

Now that you've got a basic understanding of cover and query letters, let's consider some basic vocabulary.

Literary agent: The best way to have your book published with a traditional publisher is to first send your manuscript to literary agents. These are professionals who can target your writing to the right publishers and make sure you get the best possible book deal. A literary agent looks out for your rights. To learn more about how literary agents work (and how best to work with them), read *The Writer's Relief Field Guide To Literary Agents*.

Literary journal: A literary journal, or lit mag, is a publication (in print or online) that features the work of many different writers. Some literary journals revolve around certain themes; others don't. Lit mags are rarely able to pay their writers for publication, but they are the preeminent place for up-and-coming creative writers to publish short prose and poetry. To learn more about how to get poems and creative short prose published in lit mags, read *Publishing Poetry & Prose In Literary Journals*.

Editor: An editor works at a publisher or literary journal. An editor reads submissions, acquires the rights to publish them (sometimes paying for those rights), and often edits the content. Some editors also compile and publish anthologies.

Previously published: At many literary journals, editors will not consider work that has been previously published. But as online publishing has increased, the definition of "previously published" has become murkier. For most literary journal editors, any piece that has appeared in *any* public place online (including blogs and social-network profiles) would be considered published.

With books, publishers and agents are often open to previously published (including self-published) works, as long as the writer holds all rights. When in doubt, check with the parties involved regarding their definitions and policies on what constitutes previously published work.

Simultaneous submissions: Sending the same submission to more than one editor or agent at the same time.

Multiple submissions: Sending many submissions in one letter or email to one editor or agent.

Slush pile: A stack of unsolicited submissions to book agents, literary journals, or publishing houses.

Solicited and unsolicited submissions: A solicited submission is work that an editor or literary agent has asked for. An unsolicited submission is work that an editor or literary agent has not asked for.

Masthead: The "behind the scenes" information about a publication, such as the editors, publishing information, etc.

Book reviews: Some writers pen reviews of other people's books. Literary journals will often publish those reviews, usually of the scholarly or literary variety. However, some journals are not open to book reviews from authors without a query first. Be sure to check.

Reading period: The time frame during which a given market is open to submissions. Literary agents usually accept submissions year-round. Some literary magazines don't.

Submission manager: A submission manager is an online database that manages and tracks submissions.

Word count, line count, or page count: For short prose or books, most submissions are measured in word count. Use the word count feature in your word processing program to find an estimate of your word count. Some markets will ask for works that are "no more than ten pages," in which case the word count is a bit flexible. That said, be sure you submit according to industry-standard format guidelines.

Poetry is measured in lines, not number of words. You don't have to count the title or any blank lines as "lines." Just count lines of text to get the number of lines in your poem.

Watch For These Phrases On Submission Guidelines Pages

"Do not accept genre fiction…" If a literary journal or agent says they do not accept genre fiction, this means they do not accept work that could be classified among the commercial genres, like thrillers, westerns, romances, or mysteries.

"Only previously unpublished work (or writing)." Most literary journals want first rights to a given work, and they are not interested in acquiring previously published work. Literary agents may be more open to previously published work and often like to see that excerpts from a book have been published elsewhere.

"Requires exclusivity, the exclusive right to consider the manuscript, no simultaneous submissions, or the right of first refusal." This means the literary journal or literary agent wants to be the only entity considering the work in question.

Basic Query Letter Submission Format

These are the specifications for planning your hard copy query letters sent by post (very rarely required now since most agents prefer emailed submissions):

- **One page ONLY.** No matter how tempted you are, don't send more than one page of information. It's not good form. A skilled writer should be able to summarize the salient points of a submission in one page or less. Writers who go on too long in their query letter and exceed one page could be regarded as writers who either don't know the industry etiquette, don't care to follow it, or can't master a succinct style.

- **Standard 8½" by 11" letterhead.** Avoid overly colorful paper, fancy fonts, clip art, or photos of you with your dog.

- **Clear, simple font.** While you might want to use a customized letterhead on good paper (or even a Word document laid out to look like letterhead), use a simple font like Times New Roman for the body of your letter.

- **Standard margins.** Agents know when you fuss with the margins. In our opinion, it's okay to change them a little if needed—as long as you're not setting your margins to within a hairbreadth of the edge of your page. Be moderate and you'll be fine.

- **Current contact information.** Include your mailing address, phone number, email address, and author website. Some writers who are especially active in building a following may also want to include links to their social media accounts.

- **Address** the letter to the appropriate agent. (This is where your dedicated research comes in.)

E-Letter Etiquette
Many literary agents are accepting submissions online. In fact, we've seen an enormous rise in the number of markets that prefer online communications over traditional mail.

If you are submitting an e-query letter, the same rules apply as your print letter.

Welcome To The Building Blocks of Query Letters

That means:

- You still need to keep your letter to one page even though there aren't page markers in email.
- You should include all contact info and links when possible.
- You still need your email to "look nice": no typos, good formatting.

Here are some special considerations for emailed query letters:

Your email address. If your email address is GoochieGirl or BeerLover, consider opening a new account that is a reflection of your professional goals. Choose an email address that's easy to remember; in a best-case scenario, use your real name or a combination of names and initials. We don't recommend using your pen name as your email address when submitting to agents. Pen names can change. Plus, agents want to work with *you*, not your alter ego. We'll say more on pen names later in this book.

Subject line. Use this to announce what your email message contains. (You don't want it to be mistaken for spam and deleted.) Some submissions guidelines will specify what text should be included in the subject line. If there are no specifications, we recommend a subject line such as:

- Query: Title of Book by Your Name Here.

- Query: Title of Book by Pushcart Nominee Your Name Here. (Agents like to know your literary achievements, so if you've received a major accolade, show it off succinctly in your subject line.)

- Submission: Title of Story by Your Name Here.

- Submissions: Title of One Poem Out of the Group by Your Name Here.

Salutation. In email, there's no need to use the same kind of headers (with mailing address and date) that you would use in a print letter. But even though some people feel that email can be less formal, your salutation must be professional. "Hi!" won't do.

Stationery. Again, keep it professional. Don't use background patterns, fancy fonts, dancing smiley faces, or purple text. Simple and tasteful is better.

Signature lines. Make sure to "sign" your email with your full name and contact information (phone, address). If you have an author website or social media profile, include the urls. Do not include any extra information that you might send along in your signature to friends and family, such as your favorite funny quote or a beloved image/photo.

Don't send attachments (unless the submission guidelines specifically state that attachments are allowed). If you're not sure attachments are acceptable, don't include them. Sometimes virus-scanning systems will automatically delete emails that arrive with attachments, or they will mark them as spam.

Simultaneous submissions. Sending many queries out for one given submission is fine (and far easier to do electronically), but each email should be addressed to just one recipient. It's insulting to agents to see a string of different addresses in the "To" section.

Format. Send a copy of your email to yourself to see how it looks. Did the formatting get messed up? If so, make your changes and resend yourself the letter until it looks right. You may even want to send a copy of your letter to trusted friends to ask how it appears on their computers.

Waiting for email responses. Some agents will respond to e-queries only if they're interested. Most agents who have this policy will say as much on their website. And don't be surprised if it takes months to hear back from an agent.

Part Two

Blueprint For Success

Steps To Take Before You Start Writing Your Query Letter

6 Strategies To Implement Before You Start Writing Your Query Letter

Before you even begin to write your query letter, set yourself up for success so that you can start off on the right foot. Literary agents are looking for signs that you are on your way to an exciting career that they'll want to be part of. So point them toward the possibility of a bright future with these important pre-query steps!

1. Learn how the publishing industry works. Writing a query is one thing; writing a query and understanding the way that the publishing industry works is another. Prepare to take charge of your career by learning how you fit into the larger publishing industry and also into your particular book genre. Without a good sense of the big picture, your efforts will be limited by what you don't know.

2. Create an author website. Maybe you're not ready to jump into tons of marketing and promotion for a book that you don't have published yet—and that's okay. But it's smart to have a great website ready when you begin approaching literary agents and to let them know they can find out more about you and your writing on your site.

If an agent likes your book idea, there is a very strong likelihood that he or she will check out your author website. Plus, having a website demonstrates that you are creating a foundation to support a fan base.

Full disclosure: Because we think this is such an important element of an author's success, Writer's Relief has a sister company, Web Design Relief, that specializes in budget-friendly websites just for creative writers.

3. Make connections. The publishing industry is—lucky for us—one of the few industries in which you don't necessarily need to know anybody to get published. In the end it always comes down to one thing: the writing. However, if you do a little networking with writers' organizations, you might find it's easier to get agents to seriously consider your query. Referrals from an agent's clients or colleagues will go far in moving your query letter to the top of the pile. But if you don't have any referrals, that's okay too! The important thing is to have an amazing book.

4. Rewrite your book. Once you think your book is done, go back and edit it again. Then, when it's really done, have a freelance editor take a look at it. Why frontload your efforts? If you submit the book and it doesn't get any takers, or if it has a few close calls, your attempts to revise and resubmit the book probably won't be greeted with the same enthusiasm as your initial project.

5. Build your publishing credits. As we've mentioned, it's not impossible for a writer with no publishing credentials to get a major book deal. That said, agents like to see writers who have at least a few publishing credits that will demonstrate not only a commitment to craft but also a hint of popular interest in the writing. Allow us to make a case for taking a little extra time to get a few publishing credits to your name before querying agents.

a) Being published shows agents that you can manage submission deadlines and guidelines and that you are a serious writer with serious goals. You establish yourself as savvy and in touch by being published in smaller markets, and you lay the groundwork for a career in lengthier fiction or nonfiction.

b) If editors like publishing your short works, it means they believe their readers will enjoy your writing. When an agent sees that other people are getting excited about your writing, he or she may be more likely to want in on the action.

c) Having credentials in the small press market may help you move ahead of the competition. Most agents are aware of how difficult it is to secure one single publishing credit. If an agent is offered two books of equal merit, with the only difference being that one author has a history of publishing short works and the other doesn't, you can guess which book will get the contract.

d) Not only will publishing your shorter works make you a more interesting prospect, but having those publications is emotionally rewarding. Acceptance letters from literary magazines go a long way toward keeping you motivated as you work to publish your book.

e) Publishing in literary magazines might help you directly with getting an agent. A number of our clients have been approached by big New York agencies because an agent read a client's story in a literary magazine. Getting your work, your name, and your bio out there can get you noticed. Add a blurb to your bio that you are "currently working on a novel" and see if anyone comes knocking at your door.

Now, let's return to the subject of what else you can do to create a strong foundation from which to launch your book.

6. Consider publishing an excerpt (or three!) from your book. Creating a short story or essay from within your manuscript may seem time-consuming and counterproductive, but this strategy has been very effective for many writers. Often, on the first pages of a book, you'll notice in the copyright section that the publisher wishes to acknowledge other small presses that previously printed selections from the book. Professional writers will frequently convert the first chapter of a book into a story or essay and then publish it in a literary magazine—sometimes years before the book is even finished.

How does publishing an excerpt help? The point is to be able to say in your query letter:

> *My story* "Footsteps in the Hall," *which is [based on/excerpted from] my novel* THE MONSTER KEEPER, *was published in* The Name-of-Magazine-Here Review.
>
> *My short essay* "Sue Me," *which is [based on/excerpted from] my memoir* THE MONSTER KEEPER, *was published in* Name of Newspaper Here.
>
> *My article* "Go the Extra Mile," *which is [based on/excerpted from] my self-help book* THE RUNNING ANGEL, *was published in* Name of Popular Magazine Here.

How do you choose what to excerpt? Should you pick a random chapter—or create a new story or essay based on a particular character or plot point in the book? Here are tips to creating a strong, buzzworthy book excerpt:

a) For novels or memoirs, the first chapter often works well as an excerpt. Slice-of-life moments or character sketches can also be great. Keep it simple and compelling, and make sure you aren't devoting precious space to long explanations of plot or backstory.

b) If you're writing nonfiction that isn't memoir, you might choose a particularly interesting bit from the middle of your book and see if you can find it a home in a commercial magazine (the kind on newsstands). Editors want readers to be surprised by useful or fascinating information and by your personal perspective.

c) Whatever you choose, keep your excerpt to less than 3,500 words if you want to have the largest available number of markets. You can learn more about how to get your short prose and poetry published in our book *Publishing Poetry & Prose In Literary Journals.*

d) The excerpt doesn't have to be cut word for word from your book. You can change it any way you want to fit the parameters for a short story.

e) You can also write a piece that's not in your book but one that is based on it. You may draw from material that didn't make it to the final cut or start from scratch and create a brand-new story—perhaps even a spin-off featuring a secondary character. Whatever the source, this piece should maintain the integrity of the book and stay true to the overall theme. The goal is to generate interest in the work that inspired it!

f) Choose the right ending. Compelling doesn't necessarily mean neat and tidy. Just be sure your excerpt finds some resolution or ends at a natural stopping point.

Remember, Getting A Great Book Deal Takes Time

Patience is one of the most important qualities you'll need if you want a long career as a writer. So don't shortchange yourself by skipping the key steps of laying a strong groundwork for your query letters. Even if it means delaying your queries by six months or a year, remember this: That's just the blink of an eye in the lifespan of a great book. And your project is worth it!

Approach Your Query Letter With The Right Mindset

As we stated previously in this book, a query letter is a kind of a sales pitch that agents use to decide whether or not they want to read a given manuscript.

And while we don't want to confuse the issue, it's important to note that a query is a persuasive text, not an infomercial. Grandiose and unsupportable claims, wild promises, and cutesy or overly familiar opening lines aren't going to get you very far.

In fact, *that's* what makes writing a good query so difficult—a query letter is a persuasive document that can't really *look* like it's trying to persuade anybody. All the glamour, allure, and bedazzlement have to appear effortless.

This is why we recommend taking an understated, professional approach in your query. Going for "understated" suggests that the query doesn't need excessive flash to be impressive: It's the *manuscript* itself that shines.

Again, it may help to think of your query letter as your representative on a job interview. Don't be overly formal and stuffy. You want to appear approachable, and you don't want to seem as if you're overcompensating for your book's possible shortcomings. But don't be too casual either—you wouldn't show up for an interview in your pajamas!

Also, in the same way that you would never wear a clown nose or light-up sneakers to an interview, avoid phrases and clever gambits that may come off as ploys to get attention. Clever can be annoying to agents reading letters by the thousands. If your query letter is gimmicky, literary agents may assume your book is so weak or one-note that it needs a gimmick to sell!

Literary agents want the facts—not the hype. And when you give a literary agent what he or she wants, you position yourself as a person who is professional, courteous, knowledgeable about publishing, and easy to work with.

The bottom line: Want to strike the right tone? Be straightforward, concise, and professional. Leave cute and clever to infomercials.

A Good Query Letter Is:	A Not-So-Good Query Letter Is:
Bold	Boisterous
Confident	Arrogant
Effortless	Contrived
Friendly	Pushy
Naturally Unique	Self-Infatuated
Fact-Filled	Hype-Filled

Know Thy Book: Is It Fiction? Nonfiction? Or Something Else?

One of the first things an agent will want to know when picking up your query is your book's genre. If the agent doesn't represent the genre in question, the query goes into the circular file (aka reject pile) without another moment's thought.

So getting your genre right is key.

Let's start with the most basic question:

Is the book fiction or nonfiction?

Whether your book is fiction or nonfiction will determine the type of query letter you will write and what support materials you'll need. Three basic categories are:

- Novel: fiction
- Memoir: creative nonfiction
- Popular Nonfiction: self-help, history, pop science, or how-to

Novels: The Right Genre, The Right Subgenre, The Right Word Count

Before you start writing your query, it's important to do the (sometimes difficult) work involved in pinpointing your novel genre. While there are plenty of published novels that defy all conventions of genre, it's important to represent your book as accurately and specifically as possible. To do that, you must have a firm command of the common elements of book genres.

Also, it helps to know whether or not you're within the "best practices" word count for your particular genre. If your manuscript is falling waaaay outside of the general guidelines for your genre, you might face an uphill battle trying to find a publisher willing to take on your book. If it's just a bit outside the typical word count, an agent may (or may not) be willing to work with you. It will depend on how in demand your book appears to be.

There's a lot that we could say about every single book genre out there. For now, we're going to offer you some basic pointers so you can identify your best-match book genre for your query letter. But remember: The most important thing you can do is read and read and read! Reading is the best way to acquire an intimate knowledge of your book genre.

Most novels can fall into one of three categories:
- Literary
- Mainstream/general fiction
- Genre/commercial fiction

What Is Literary Fiction? How Do You Know If Your Book Qualifies As Literary?

Literary fiction is fiction of ideas. While the story must be good, emphasis on action is not often as important as emphasis on the ideas, themes, and concerns of the book. Literary fiction tackles issues that are often controversial, difficult, and complex.

Aside from subject matter, literary fiction tends to be written with emphasis on prose style. While genre fiction is "transparent" (readers can see through the text to escape into the story itself), literary writers want the reader to notice how beautiful the writing is. Sometimes the writing prevents the reader from escaping into the story, but that's not a bad thing in this genre.
Literary fiction is very specialized and difficult to do well. Literary readers (especially readers of experimental and "high literary" forms) are very demanding and are usually considered a niche market.

What Is General Fiction? How Do You Know If Your Book Qualifies As Mainstream?

Mainstream fiction, which goes by many other names (general fiction, upmarket, and literary light), is driven by a mix of genre fiction and literary fiction techniques. In mainstream fiction, the writer must have a strong "hook" or premise. The story must be readable, with a somewhat traditional plot arc, and be plot- and character-driven.

Mainstream fiction tends to blend transparent language with occasional bouts of prose that feel more literary in tone. Writers of general fiction can have a variety of voices and write in a variety of styles, but all are accessible and not too experimental.

However, keep in mind that the boundaries between the genres can be blurred. One person's literary novel might be another person's mainstream book.

How Long Is A Literary Novel? How Long Is A Mainstream Novel?

A literary novel can be between 40,000 and 120,000 words long. If you're a new writer, literary agents and editors will likely want to see a novel between 70,000 and 100,000 words. A mainstream novel is usually best-suited when it hits the 70K-100K mark as well.

Commercial Fiction And Genre Fiction

Genre fiction refers to books that are published widely for popular appeal. Usually genre books are published in the smaller, mass-market book size.

Genre Guidelines

The following information is an overview of *generalized* genre guidelines: Always research information about your specific project for the best results. Some industry pundits might have slight variations on these recommendations, so follow your instincts and your muse. Also, remember that some authors have tackled "commercial" genres with huge "literary" success.

Romance Novels
A romance novel offers a love story that ends with a happily ever after. The central characters are the hero and heroine, and the central conflict is about negotiating successful terms for their relationship.

A single title (or stand-alone) romance novel runs between 80,000 and 100,000 words. A category romance novel (like those published by Harlequin) is generally shorter, and each "line" or "imprint" will have its own strict specifications. Save yourself a lot of trouble: Research before you write!

Subgenres of romance include paranormal, erotica, Regency, historical, contemporary, women's fiction, Christian, time travel, fantasy/science fiction, and more.

Women's Fiction
Women's fiction novels tend to be stories that focus on intense emotions and relationships. Family troubles, friendships, the rigors of growing older, and the courage to pursue forgotten dreams are all fodder for women's fiction. Women's fiction can feature a romantic element, but the romance is not necessarily the driving force of the book.

Women's fiction novels tend to be between 80,000 and 100,000 words. At the time of this writing, women's fiction can be either historical or contemporary.

Fantasy Novels
Create the parameters of your fantasy world in advance and stick to them. Design the environment (geography, weather), the characters (race, creatures), and other details such as the use of magic, the history of your environment (wars, etc.), and limitations of powers.

How long are fantasy novels? Between 80,000 and 150,000+ words (approximately). They can be longer than traditional published novels and are sometimes serialized.

Subgenres of fantasy include alternate history, urban, dark, high, historical, steampunk, wuxia, fantasy of manners, and more.

Westerns
Westerns should be set in the Old West (west of the Mississippi River and before the year 1900). Historical details should be accurate.

Westerns tend to be on the shorter side of fiction books, anywhere from 45,000 to 75,000 words.

Historical Fiction
Though there is quite a lot of debate on the definition, "historical" can generally mean that the story takes place at least fifty years in the past. Careful research is especially important.

Generally, a stand-alone historical may be 85,000 to 100,000 words. For first-time writers, submitting a book longer than 100,000 words is especially difficult, but historical novels have been known to be on the long side. They can fall anywhere on the spectrum of literary fiction, mainstream fiction, and genre fiction.

Mystery Novels
Create a solvable puzzle for your readers—mystery novels are supposed to be fun to read and fun to solve, but if the reader isn't provided with plausible clues to follow, they'll lose interest.

Mysteries vary in length depending on subgenre. Single-title mysteries may be between 75,000 and 100,000 words. Cozy mysteries, like those in a mystery series, may be on the shorter side.

Subgenres of mystery include hardboiled, supernatural, crime, true crime, amateur sleuth, police procedural, cozy, and more. Be certain of whether you are writing a mystery or a thriller.

Thrillers
Thrillers are designed to do one thing: thrill. Strong characters, tight plots, and an emphasis on action over flowery prose drive this genre to daring storylines. Thrillers often feature determined protagonists and clear antagonists, and they can be set in nearly any location imaginable. They can be graphic (gritty) or somewhat more subtle, but focus is always on suspense. Thrillers often incorporate a mystery element.

Thriller novels hit the genre-standard sweet spot of 90,000 to 100,000 words for new writers. Thrillers tend to go a little longer as well.

Subgenres of thrillers include action, conspiracy, disaster, crime, eco, political, erotic, psychological, legal, and more.

Horror
Horror novels capitalize on fears and phobias; the supernatural and paranormal are welcome. Horror can be violent or gory to varying degrees.

Horror novels vary in length, but generally, a stand-alone novel will be between 80,000 and 100,000 words.
Subgenres of horror include psychological, ghost, weird menace, erotic, body horror, occult detective, and more.

Science Fiction
Science fiction blends science and technology that push our imaginations to the limit with elements of reality. Sci-fi novels tend to explore alternative possibilities and are often filled with thoughtful commentary.

Science fiction novels can vary in length, but generally speaking, a stand-alone sci-fi novel may be between 90,000 and 120,000 words.

Subgenres include hard, soft, cyberpunk, space western, alternate history, space opera, military, and more.

Young Adult (YA)
Young adult fiction targets an audience between the ages of 12 and 18. The tone, style, and content of YA novels change significantly depending on the specific age a writer is targeting.

YA novels vary in length depending on demographic, but generally run between 40,000 and 100,000 words or more, depending on the targeted age group.

Subgenres of YA include most of the same subgenres of adult fiction. "Edgy" YA tackles especially controversial or difficult issues.

New Adult
New adult features protagonists in their twenties who are transitioning from young adulthood to full adulthood. New adult fiction can often be more explicit than young adult fiction in terms of violence and sex.

New adult fiction can range anywhere from 80,000 words to 100,000 words.

Still Don't Know Your Book Genre?

Sometimes a writer simply doesn't know what genre his or her book fits into. And while it certainly can help your cause if your book fits neatly into a single genre, don't lose hope if your book isn't so cut-and-dried.

The Dangers Of Overly Obscure Book Genres

The number of book genres and subgenres out there is dizzying (especially for novels!). For certain books, pigeonholing a project into a genre that's too narrow or obscure might suggest to literary agents that there isn't a big market for it.

The Dangers Of Overly Broad Book Genres

If you write in your query letter: *Please consider my 100,000-word adventure, sci-fi romance with a touch of steampunk that may be suitable for young adults and adults because it appeals to everyone*, then an agent or editor might think, *How on earth can I market this book successfully? There's no niche.*

Rather than boasting in your query letter, *Everyone will love this book*, think: *Who is the best reader for my particular kind of novel? If I were in a bookstore, which shelf would this sit on?*

That's your genre.

What To Do If Your Genre Is Mixed

Sometimes the distinction between book genres can be hard to determine. For example: A women's fiction novel may have as its centerpiece a strong romantic story. Is it romance? Is it women's fiction?

If you think your book genre is romance and a potential agent thinks it is women's fiction, there may be some unwanted friction or misunderstandings—especially if the agent thinks the book genre label you picked doesn't fit your actual book!

When you're pitching a book and you're not certain of the genre, it may be best to simply not include a specific genre in your letter and leave it to the agent to decide.

What matters is that the agent likes the book—regardless of genre. If an agent likes it, he or she will help you figure out the best place to position it. Just be sure that the blurb or mini-synopsis in your query letter is well-written and provides an idea of the direction of your book.

To some extent, the genre of your book can depend less on what's between the pages and more on what a publisher decides to do for marketing and positioning. Don't write off genre entirely. But don't stress too much about it either. Read books that will help you write good books. That's what matters.

Memoir: The 4 Pre-Query Factors That Will Influence Your Success

Many people write memoirs. And we love that: We believe that sharing our stories with one another truly does make the world a better place. All memoirs—whether they are dramatic stories surrounding well-known events or quiet stories of growing up during a certain era—deserve to be written and read.

That said, when literary agents are looking for a memoir that is going to be a big, commercial success, there are a few key factors that can influence the level of their enthusiasm.

The Celebrity Factor

If you're on the A-list, you'll get a book deal. Nuff said.

If elements of your personal story have been covered by local or national news media, or if you've been interviewed, featured, or honored as a result of your life experience, that publicity will go a long way toward drumming up enthusiasm for your memoir.

But if the only camera pointed at you is on your own cell phone, that doesn't mean you have no shot at nabbing a book deal for a memoir. It just means that your story has to be exceptionally compelling. If you're not famous, then your life story has to be big, emotional, and fascinating enough to *make* you famous—or at least famous enough to sell a fair number of copies of your book.

The Uniqueness Factor

The most important element of a memoir written by an average Joe/Jane is the content of the story. What makes your memoir special? What about it will get readers' pulses racing? What will make them say, "I can't believe this is true!"?

If you're worried that your story isn't unusual enough to be picked up by a big publisher, don't fabricate or exaggerate to make your life seem more exciting. While there's a place in this world for shocking and flashy memoirs, stories about "regular life" can also strike a chord with readers. Some of the best memoirs are the "quiet" ones, the stories that move us to cry or smile. Readers enjoy stories by people who are grappling with the fundamental human conundrums we all face. Just write the most emotional, insightful, entertaining, and authentic book that you can. *That's* what makes your story unique.

The Craft Factor

A good story told badly is a bad story. So your writing must do justice to the story of your life. It can take years to learn the craft of good writing (some say it takes 10,000 hours). If you're not certain that you are writing at a very high level, consider working with a ghostwriter, line editor, or content editor. Don't rely on a literary agent or publisher to brush up your manuscript for you. Your memoir must be complete and polished prior to submission to literary agents.

The Readership Factor

There are two ways of approaching this question. The first is impersonal. If you've written a memoir about birding, then you know you have a potential readership among the country's dedicated birders—you don't need to dedicate yourself to *creating* a new trend in bird-watching. Agents will love knowing that there's a preexisting audience for your subject matter.

The second way of approaching this question is personal: What have *you* been doing that will suggest to agents there will be interest in your memoir? Are you blogging to a substantial audience who loves to read posts based on your real-life experiences? Have you been asked to be a speaker because of your experiences? Would you be willing to become a speaker if your memoir takes off? Memoir writers do not *need* to develop an author platform in the same way that an author of popular nonfiction needs to. But every little bit helps.

The Bottom Line For Pitching A Memoir

Many memoirs are written every year; few get book deals with traditional publishers. If being a commercial success or spreading the word about your experience to the masses is your intention, we recommend you do everything you can to put together a compelling reason for agents and editors to say YES to your book. Good luck!

Nonfiction Query Letters: How To Prepare Before You Query

If you're writing any kind of nonfiction other than a memoir (like a book about how to raise kids or the history of football), then most of the work you'll need to do to get a major publisher will happen even *before* you start writing your query letter.

Without proper pre-query preparation, we can almost guarantee that your query letter will be ineffective. In order to generate interest in your nonfiction self-help or how-to book, you've GOT to show literary agents that you have a strong author platform.

What Is An Author Platform?

Literary agents and editors use the word "platform" within the publishing industry to talk about an author's relationship with his or her audience.

Writers of both fiction and nonfiction can have strong author platforms, but it's especially important for nonfiction authors.

Author Platforms In Real Life

An author's platform involves many components: the author's expertise in the field that he or she is writing about; the author's preexisting popularity, notoriety, and status as a leader in his or her field; and the author's personal, already established connection to the readership who will be interested in his or her book.

In short, a platform is the author's background within a given field that establishes him or her as the right person to publish (and sell) a book on the subject.

Most of the time, writers of self-help, how-to, or even biography proposals will need a strong platform.

What Is A Strong Platform? A Weak Platform?

Let's say you've written a nonfiction book proposal to publish a book about a brand-new weight-loss diet: *The Lima Bean Diet*.

An author who has a strong platform:

- Is a highly educated nutritionist with multiple degrees and special studies about lima beans.

- Has written and published many peer-reviewed articles on lima beans in science journals.

- Has written and published many popular weight-loss articles about lima beans in major commercial magazines.

- Has a website and blog with a strong following of people who have had success with The Lima Bean Diet.

- Has gained some preliminary media coverage (local TV spots, articles, interviews) that suggests The Lima Bean Diet is the next big thing.

- Has led seminars all over the nation about The Lima Bean Diet and has a growing mailing list.

- Is very Googleable: When an agent does a Web search on the author's name, there are multiple results for The Lima Bean Diet.

A writer who has a weak platform:

- Has minimal or informal education in his or her field and relies on personal experience to prove The Lima Bean Diet works.

- Has published a few articles on The Lima Bean Diet in "underground" blogs, websites, and zines.

- Has not published anything in commercial magazines or has published only in small-circulation periodicals.

- Has a blog but not many followers—and few of the followers are active.

- Has a following of family, friends, friends of friends—but that's where it ends.

- Has had little to no media coverage.

- Has no reputation for being an expert; leads a couple of local seminars in libraries or health-food stores.

- Appears once or twice when a Web search is done, but otherwise isn't active online.

What Your Platform Means To A Literary Agent Or Editor

Nonfiction writing is especially competitive. Many people believe that their personal experiences alone make them the authority on their subject—but that's not the case. To make "big numbers" on a nonfiction book, a literary agent will look for an author who has a built-in audience of readers who depend on and trust the author's expertise.

Rarely, a literary agent may be willing to work with an author to build up a platform in order to impress an editor—but these instances are few and far between.

How To Build Up A Better Platform For Your Writing

1. Be (or become) an expert in your field.

2. Establish a strong online presence.

3. Write articles for major commercial magazines.

4. Speak as an expert and leader.

5. Offer seminars and establish yourself as a speaker.

6. Hire a publicist who can help with media exposure.

The strength of your author platform should be obvious in the bio section of your query letter, as well as in the bio section of your book proposal (more on that later). When you have a strong platform, you will also have an amazing bio that will show literary agents you've got a winning book on your hands.

7 Easy Ways To Build Your Reputation For Your Book Query

If the philosopher Descartes was around today, he might have said: "I'm Googleable, therefore I am."

Okay—maybe he wouldn't have said exactly those words. But the point is, if a writer wants to make a name for himself or herself, being search-engine accessible is important. While we could write a whole book about how to build your reputation as a writer, we'll review the most important points for you here.

For nonfiction, your reputation counts big. So take the time to create a strong platform before you start querying. Then, be sure to feature your platform in your author bio.

Here are a few basic ways to make your name appear more frequently in search engine results:

1. Develop an author website. Make sure your author website is search-engine optimized. At the very least, mention your name numerous times on your website. TIP: Update your content regularly. Search engines like that.

2. Join social networks. We know there are only so many social networks one person can effectively maintain. But if you can pick two, and create profiles (updating them occasionally), your social networks should begin to show up in Web searches. For the best results, we recommend hiring a social media assistant. Writer's Relief offers a Virtual Assistant program that can maintain and update your social media accounts for you.

3. Focus on online literary journals and magazines. With each online publication that gives you a byline, search engines return that result. In a perfect world, a literary agent or editor will Google your name and find examples of your writings on reputable websites.

4. Be picture-perfect. When posting your picture on your website, tag your photo with your name so that Google will associate your image with your name. Use your name in the file name, the title of the photo, the alternative text, and the description (you can access these things by clicking "editing -> advanced" if you're in WordPress). Then, when agents or editors Google you, your headshot will show in search results.

5. Ask friends to review your work. Ask fellow bloggers or social network friends to review your writing. When they use your name online, it may show up in searches. Just be sure not to offend anyone by making your request in an inappropriate or pushy way.

6. Blog. Your recent blog posts should show up in search results. Hint: Try using your own name in your blog posts if they're not showing up otherwise. You can always sign your posts with your name, if you like.

7. Post a video of yourself on YouTube. Google owns YouTube. Which means Google likes YouTube. Which means YouTube videos frequently show up in search results. So post a little video and tag it using your name in the keywords and description. And if you happen to get hit in the face with a pie, even better—because your video might go viral!

Part Three

The Nuts And Bolts Of Your Novel And Memoir Query Letter

The 5 Common Elements Of Novel And Memoir Query Letters

Let's review the sections that every query letter must have. The first five we will discuss are:

1. Salutation
2. Introduction to the work
3. Book blurb/summary
4. Author bio
5. Closing lines

Element #1: Greetings And Salutations!

No matter how certain you may be that Lou and Pat are females (or males!), you should not assume the sex of the reader. In order to avoid embarrassing yourself and alienating a potential ally, follow what has become the industry standard rule for addressing decision-makers:

Simply use the first *and* last name of the literary agent to whom you are sending your submission, *without* a Mr. or Mrs. salutation (example: Dear Pat Doe; Dear Lou Smith). We know what you're thinking: The only time you ever hear your full name this way involves telemarketers. But because the strategy is useful and gender-neutral, it is now standard business protocol for professional correspondence.

Using an agent's first and last name for your submissions won't be held against you. But if you address a literary agent by the wrong gender, you're definitely starting out on the wrong foot.

Element #2: Put Your Best Line Forward: Introduce Your Book The Right Way

First impressions happen in an instant. Many new writers look at the first line of their query letter as if it's the first line of an infomercial or one of those local car commercials in which the dealership owner is dressed like Abe Lincoln and yelling waaaay too loud: *Get down here TODAY for the BEST deals of the CENTURY!* Most of us change the channel or hit mute. Make an overblown grab for attention in the first line of your query, and agents might instantly think, *Why does this writer need a gimmick to get my attention?*

Again, we remind you that a good query letter is quietly confident, not desperately needy. And that's why we believe that, when in doubt, an understated approach works best—especially in the first lines.

Most of the time, writers are querying literary agents whom they haven't personally met. And that's okay! Cold-call queries can be successful queries. Generally, we find that the best way to nail your cold-call intro is to keep it simple. Offer the key information right up front, like genre, word count, and title:

- Please consider my 80,000-word women's fiction novel, *Go For Broke.*

- I hope you'll be interested in learning more about my self-help book *Go For Broke*; the proposal is ready for review, and I expect the book to be completed (at 80,000 words) in six months.

- I hope you'll consider requesting sample pages of my 80,000-word memoir, *Go For Broke.*

- I believe that your interest in books with strong female characters might make my 80,000-word women's fiction novel, *Go For Broke*, a good fit at your literary agency.

If you can take a personal approach to reach out to an agent you met (perhaps at a writing conference), feel free to do so. Jog the agent's memory with a reminder about how you know each other so he or she can connect the query letter with your face.

- You and I met at the Name of Writers Conference last week; I was the one wearing the Scottish terrier earrings that you liked so much.

> We didn't have much time to chat when we were in line for the dinner buffet, so I wanted to touch base to see if you would be interested in my 80,000-word women's fiction novel, *Go For Broke*.

If you met the agent at a "speed dating" session at a writing conference (when agents and writers sit down to chat for ten minutes), remind the agent of your connection. If you talked for ten minutes about your storyline, the agent will likely connect your name and face without additional prompting. But if something memorable happened during your session, feel free to refer to it to jog the agent's memory. Just don't wait too long after your meeting to send your query or follow-up materials so the agent doesn't forget who you are!

- It was great meeting you at the Name of Conference last week; I'm so glad you were interested in seeing the first twenty pages of my 80,000-word women's fiction novel, *Go For Broke*.

- I'm so glad we got to meet at Name of Conference last week; it was a lot of fun discovering that we both have unruly Dalmatians! Per your request, I'm submitting sample pages of my 80,000-word women's fiction novel, *Go For Broke*. Before you take a look, let me remind you of the premise and of my author bio.

If you haven't met any literary agents, but can make a connection based on someone you know or admire, you can try this approach:

- Your client Writer's Name Here and I are both members of Name of Writing organization, and she recently suggested that you might like to take a look at my 80,000-word women's fiction novel, *Go For Broke*.

- Your client Name Here has always been one of my favorite writers, so when I was considering which agency might best represent my 80,000-word women's fiction novel, *Go For Broke*, I thought of you.

If your book lends itself to summary easily, you might consider including a little more description right off the bat—and that means taking a cue from the movie industry and repurposing a log line for your own use.

A log line is a very short description of the characters and main action of your book. If used appropriately, a log line or brief summary in the beginning of your query letter will capture not only the story of your book, but also the essential energy and momentum.

Here's an example:

- Please consider my 90,000-word science fiction novel, *Night Storm*, the story of a shy fifteen-year-old boy who must save his small Midwestern town after a mysterious thunderstorm causes his father and others to go missing.

Self-help and how-to books can also benefit from a brief description in the first line of a query letter. When a how-to or self-help book's intention isn't clear from the title, a short description can help:

- I hope you'll be intrigued by the proposal for my book *Breaking The Rules*, which teaches people how to free themselves from years of ingrained bad habits.

Seems easy enough, right?

The trouble with introducing your book with a summary in your query letter's first line is that it's really hard to do well. And if you start with a not-so-great opening line, you might lose your reader's interest before he or she even gets to the second sentence.

Here's an example of a bad log line for a novel:

- Please consider my 90,000-word science fiction novel, *Night Storm*, a story of alien abductions during thunderstorms, father-son relationships, and a boy's quest to save the world.

In the above example, each element of the book's plot is presented in a way that feels more "noun-y" than "verb-y." There's no momentum.

Here's another bad one:

- Please consider my 90,000-word science fiction novel, *Night Storm*, about a kid who has to save his father after he disappears.

Can you see what's wrong with this one? It fails to capture the unique elements of the story or the emotional impact of the hero's journey.

And another bad one:

- Please consider my 90,000-word science fiction novel, *Night Storm*, which chronicles what happens when a thunderstorm comes to a

Midwestern town, causing people to disappear, including the hero's father.

This doesn't give us a picture of the characters, the nature of the town, or the intensity of the action. Plus, it's very wordy and doesn't make a crisp, emotional point.

One more bad one for the road:

- Please consider my 90,000-word science fiction novel, *Night Storm,* a story of fathers, sons, growing up in America, and learning to be a hero.

This first line focuses too heavily on theme instead of story. In a good query, theme comes through *via* story (not apart from it). The theme shouldn't have to be stated so obviously if it's already apparent from the action.

Last bad one:

- Please consider my 90,000-word science fiction novel, *Night Storm,* a story of fathers, sons, growing up in America, and learning to be a hero when a young wallflower teenager boy realizes that a freak thunderstorm is actually an alien invasion, and he must rescue his father and save his town.

Aside from being poorly worded, this example is much too long. Your query letter's first line needs to be tight and punchy to work.

There is absolutely nothing wrong with taking a simple approach in your opening line.

A bad first line descriptive phrase:

- Offers vague or unclear information in a way that isn't intriguing.

- Presents dull, isolated facts, as opposed to an exciting story.

- Focuses too heavily on themes instead of action and character. (Example: *A story of love and determination during World War II.*)

- Goes on too long or just doesn't grab readers. Some books simply don't lend themselves well to summary, and forcing the issue can hurt more than it helps.

Query Chestnuts: The 3 Types Of Opening Lines That Rarely Work

Excerpted quotes from characters, or descriptive passages. Some writers pick out a favorite passage from their book and plunk it down right at the beginning of the query letter. We don't recommend this strategy. Few agents will wade through your character's speech to get information (genre, title, word count) that the query letter should have started with.

Plus, just because a certain snippet resonates with you doesn't mean it will resonate the same way with agents. As the writer, you have an emotional attachment to the characters and the action. Agents don't. And it's rare that a line (or three) will instantly create a deep level of attachment.

The rhetorical question. You've seen this angle before: *What would you do if you discovered your spouse was cheating?* Or *What would you do if you were a trained assassin, and your next target was your best friend?* Unless your rhetorical question is really good, skip it. The "cheating spouse" angle has been explored ad infinitum—so this rhetorical question doesn't add anything new. And few people ever think of themselves as trained assassins. Only use a rhetorical question that is engaging in a very specific and emotionally surprising way.

The big promise. Some writers will start their queries with a wildly spectacular statement: *My book,* Title Here, *is the next* Harry Potter, *the next* Hunger Games, *the next* Gone Girl—*and I hope you'll get back to me ASAP to let me know if you'll want it before Oprah does.* Agents are unimpressed—and a bit put off—by hubris; don't give agents a negative impression of you or your book in the very first line!

Is A Log Line Right For Your Query Letter?

If you want to try for a log line-esque summary in the first lines of your query, be sure you focus on what's surprising and magnetic about your story. Then write your descriptive phrase over and over again until you get it exactly right.

And if you're even a little concerned that your log line might not be deeply compelling—just leave it out. Better to start your query letter with a simple statement of the facts than to hurt your chances with a first line that flops.

Comparing Your Book To Similar Titles In Your Query Letter

Some authors start their queries by offering examples of similar book titles early on.

- *Please consider my 80,000-word memoir,* Footloose And Fancy-Free, *a travel memoir of trail-hiking and personal growth along the lines of* Lost *and* A Walk In The Woods.

This often-touted tactic isn't *bad*, but it can be dangerous in the wrong hands.

First, we'll give you the potential dangers of offering agents comparable book titles. Then, we'll teach you the *right* way of mentioning similar books so you can avoid those dangers.

Caution: Here's Why You Should Think Twice About Making Comparisons

Comparing your book to a well-known title. You know that book everybody's reading right now? You can bet the market is filled with query letters promising to be *just like that book*. But here's the problem: That book's already been written. And since everybody's query letters are comparing to that book, *your* book could be shrugged off as another copycat.

Comparing to overly obscure titles. Dangerous as it is to compare your book to the most popular book on the *New York Times* list, it's equally as dangerous to compare to a book that's not well-known. If you compare your title to another that didn't have good sales numbers, your effort might backfire.

Comparing to the wrong titles. As a writer, it can be hard to "see" your own book. So we've seen countless writers compare their books to titles that don't quite match up or make sense. And that can weaken your branding and positioning.

Connecting books that have nothing in common. Some writers try to choose two titles that are very different in hopes of stimulating an agent to consider a new idea based on "formulas" that already work—*It's like* The Da Vinci Code *meets* Gone With The Wind! *It's like* Lost *meets* A Million Little Pieces. *It's like* The 7 Habits Of Highly Effective People *meets* Rich Dad, Poor Dad.

We've seen this angle backfire many times, because often the crossed titles end up being more confusing than clarifying.

What if you compare your book to a book the agent hates? Let's say Agent A reads only a book blurb, loves the idea, and asks for sample pages. Meanwhile, Agent B has exactly the same taste as Agent A, reads the same book blurb, but also reads that the author has compared the story to a book the agent hates. That's a missed opportunity waiting to happen—especially if the comparison wasn't really a good one to begin with!

Comparing Titles For Nonfiction

If you compare nonfiction, know that you're up against the same odds as a writer who compares fiction. If you skimmed the previous section, now's the moment to go back and read it.

But the "comparing game" changes a bit when we move into the realm of prescriptive nonfiction or popular nonfiction. If your nonfiction book is in a field that is saturated, you may want to point to other titles to demonstrate how your book is different from what's already out there. Otherwise, it may not be obvious to an agent why your book called *How To Grow A Garden* is different than any other garden book on the shelves.

If You Are Going To Compare Book Titles In Your Query...

Let's be clear. We're not saying you should never compare. When done correctly, book comparisons can be helpful to agents. Literary agents like to see that writers are intimately familiar with their book genres. And well-done comparisons can be very useful when an agent is trying to get a sense of what the submitted book might be like.

Here are some things to do before you include a line about book comparisons in your query:

- If you're writing on a subject that really has no comparisons, don't "force" a comparison that isn't a natural fit. Comparisons aren't mandatory in queries.

- Run your comparisons past other book lovers or writing group members who are familiar with your book. Do they think your book compares appropriately? Do they have other suggestions?

- If you're going to cross-reference, see if your "A meets B" concept is clear, precise, and easy to envision. Ask others what they think: Do they understand *exactly* what your comparison means? Or are they confused about which elements, exactly, are overlapping?

- Consider the popularity or obscurity of the comparison. If you are going to compare to a wildly popular and trendy book, do so carefully and explain how your book is different. If you're going to compare to an obscure book, make a case for why *your* book could be more effectively marketed.

Element #3: The Book Blurb (Or Summary) For Your Novel Or Memoir

The book blurb is one of the main differences between cover letters and query letters. In short, a book blurb is a descriptive summary of your book, whether it's fiction or nonfiction.

In this section, we're going to focus on how to write a blurb for a memoir or a novel. Although memoirs are nonfiction and novels are fiction, the two forms have a lot in common—especially when it comes to query letters. Both genres offer stories populated by interesting characters who have fascinating adventures. Both memoirs and novels must be totally complete before a query is submitted to a literary agent. For that reason, we've grouped novels and memoirs together when discussing query letters. When we say "character," we're referring not only to characters in novels, but to any "character" in a memoir.

If your book falls somewhere between a novel and a memoir, and you're not sure how to best position it, please first skip to Part Six—Custom Designs For Special Query Letters to learn more about mixed genre writing. Then return here so we can get back to creating your query letter book blurb!

A good query blurb is exciting, energetic, succinct, and magnetic. It's like the description of a book on the back cover or dust flap; it's meant to tantalize and intrigue readers to make them want more.

But don't try to cram every last detail into your query's book blurb: Include *only* those elements that are going to make a person want to read your book. It's not about writing a summary that's exhaustive and complete; it's about writing a summary that's engaging, leading, and persuasive.

If an agent is intrigued by your summary, he or she may ask that you send all or part of the manuscript, as well as a synopsis. A synopsis is a summary of a book (usually one to two pages) that gives the agent a more detailed picture of your book's plot and characters. We'll talk more about your synopsis in a later section.

How long is a book blurb? Usually around 150 words; we almost never go longer than 200 words. That means packing a lot of punch in a little package.

Query Letter Book Summary Template: Fill In The Blanks To Write A Great Summary!

The first step in summarizing your story is deciding what's most important for readers to know. Our step-by-step worksheet will help you determine the key elements of your book so you can focus on what matters in your story and let the rest go. In case you're skipping around as you read, please note that this worksheet works best for novels and memoirs.

Also, keep in mind that the only way to master the tropes of your particular genre is to read many summaries of books in that genre. Does your particular book genre have any patterns that become evident when you read several dozen summaries? If so, you might want to consider sticking with what works.

Let's get started. Grab some paper or your computer and write short descriptions of the following story elements so you can identify the most important points to cover in your query letter.

SETTING:
Describe your setting using your most evocative and succinct language. Does your setting directly influence the *main* action of your story? If so, how?
- What's your story's year or time period?
- Pick three adjectives that describe your time and place.

MAIN CHARACTER:
Who is your main character? We understand that some books have multiple protagonists. But since you've only got a couple hundred words—if that—for your summary, we recommend focusing on the character who has the most to lose because of the main conflict. If you're writing an ensemble cast book, read further.
- Pick three adjectives or phrases that describe the main character's personality.
- In one vivid sentence describe the main character's life and problems—or apparent lack thereof—just before the book opens.
- Describe the plot event that changes the character's life as he/she knows it when the book begins.
- Describe the way the character must alter plans/goals/expectations because of the event.
- Describe what/who stands in the way of your character's main goal—the antagonist or antagonistic force.
- Describe what your character will lose if he/she does not achieve the objective.
- Describe physical dangers, if any.

SECONDARY CHARACTERS:
Who in the main character's life complicates/helps/changes the situation the most? How are this person's goals opposite from/different than the main character's goals?
- Describe that person in three short phrases or words, then state his/her role—the way he/she changes key events.

THE CLIMACTIC MOMENT:
In a query for a traditionally plotted story, the end of the book blurb should be a very leading, very tantalizing hint of some final showdown/standoff/dark moment. The query doesn't give away the ending, but it points to an ending that will force the main character to put everything on the line in one way or another. In other words, the last lines of your book blurb should entice your reader to want to know what happens. The following questions will help you crystallize your strategy.

Think about:
- What does your character learn at the end of the book?
- What does your character achieve at the end of the book?

And now:
- Describe the way the character is moving closer to (or further from) his/her goals. Then…
- Describe the low point. This "dark moment" is usually where your query blurb trails off, leaving the reader to wonder if the character will find his/her way out of peril in order to succeed. The darker the dark moment, the better!
- Describe what the character must learn/discover/overcome/achieve to succeed. But be sure to make it clear that success is not guaranteed. Tease the reader with the promise of a great ending!

Now you know which elements are most important to your query. The key is organizing them in a way that is both succinct and compelling!

A Useful Structure For Summarizing Your Book's Story

Let's take apart a familiar story to see how the blurb might look.

The example we've deconstructed below is based on fiction, but you can use this method for memoirs as well by laying out your main action in the same way. The primary difference is that a memoir-writer will use first person POV, not third.

In the movie version of *The Wizard of Oz*, Dorothy is the main character. She and her three companions all have something to lose (their lives) and something to gain (a heart, a brain, etc.), but of the four, Dorothy has the *most* to lose—she is in the "wrong" world and must get back to Kansas. So in your synopsis, the story should unfold through Dorothy's perspective. Focus on her and focus all the action through her.

Once you've identified your main character, ask yourself these questions to pinpoint the main conflict:

What does the character risk externally—her house, his life, her job, his favorite T-shirt?

- *Her life. There's a witch who wants to kill her.*

What does the character risk internally—her heart, his friendship, her mother's respect, his children's admiration?

- *If she doesn't get back to Kansas, she'll never see her family again. And she's only just realized how important they are to her.*

These are the two main points of conflict that should be filtered through your main character's point of view in your query letter.

Now, let's look at one possible structure for laying out the action.

1. Set the mood. If your book is set in a great locale, take a phrase or even a sentence to describe it. If the setting doesn't matter much and your book happens to be action-oriented, then set the mood by diving right into the action.

And if your book has a great setting that is inherently linked to the main conflict, well...

- *Dorothy, a young girl who longs for a different life, is whisked away from her dull Kansas farm into the magical, colorful world of Oz when her house is carried off in a tornado.*

2. Identify the key conflicts in concrete terms. Show us what your character stands to lose using his or her viewpoint, and you'll have great emotional impact.

- *Only the Wizard of Oz, magician of the Emerald City, has the power to send Dorothy home. She and three new friends—a scarecrow, a tin man, and a lion—make their way down the yellow brick road toward the Wizard's castle.*

3. Show advancing, specific action (but not too much). Once the main conflict has been identified, tell us one or two major things that stand in the way of the character's success.

- *Dorothy inadvertently makes an enemy of the wicked witch, so her quest to find the Wizard becomes a matter of life and death. But the Wizard isn't interested in giving handouts: He won't help Dorothy and her friends unless they first kill the powerful witch who pursues them.*

4. Lead the reader up to the climactic moment. Don't give away the ending. Instead, bring the climactic elements into clear focus, then keep us guessing.

- *Will Dorothy, who never appreciated her home until now, make it back to Kansas with her life?*

Here's how the blurb would look in paragraph form:

- *Dorothy, a young girl who longs for a different life, is whisked away from her dull Kansas farm into the magical, colorful world of Oz when her house is carried away by a tornado. When the house lands on the Wicked Witch of the West and kills her, Dorothy makes a deadly enemy of her sister, the Wicked Witch of the East. Only the Wizard of Oz, magician of the Emerald City, has the power to save Dorothy by sending her home. She and three new friends—a scarecrow, tin man, and lion—make their way down the yellow brick road toward the Wizard's castle. But the Wizard isn't interested in giving handouts: He won't help Dorothy and her friends unless they first kill the powerful wicked witch who pursues them. Will Dorothy,*

> *who never appreciated her home until now, make it back to Kansas with her life?*

You can see how this method works for sketching out your query letter blurb. This will not work for every book, but using this method may give you some insight into the best way to lay out a blurb for your story.

You'll notice that we had to leave a lot of things out of this query summary. There's no mention of ruby slippers or Toto. We don't give away the Wizard's secret identity. We don't talk about Munchkins or Glinda or even the killing of the Wicked Witch of the East.

We love those elements—we really do! But a query writer must strike the right balance between detail and action. And that means leaving some things out.

Alternative Book Blurbs: Sagas, Ensemble Casts, And Literary Stories

Some books don't lend themselves to the traditional summary style we've outlined because the stories themselves are not traditional in terms of rising action, climax, and denouement. So the template we just explained can be informative—but there's no use trying to pound a square peg into a round hole. You'll need to take a different approach.

SAGAS follow many characters over a long period of time, with lots of storylines going at once. To summarize a saga, a writer has to play up the elements that make it interesting: the dramatic characters, the vivid setting, the time period, the immersive world of the story. You can choose a single character as the focus, using him/her as the axis for the action and as the lens through which we see all of the other characters. Or you can touch on each of the characters, with an emphasis on their collaborative plight.

Here's an example of a saga blurb that touches on each of the characters:

> *Across The Line* tells the interwoven stories of the Efkens, an 1860s family of immigrants who have fallen on hard times and decide to try their luck in the harsh prairies of the Nebraska frontier. The family's patriarch, John, struggles with the sense that he has failed his family, leading him to change from a warmhearted father into a domineering and fearful tyrant. His perpetually pregnant wife, Emily, does her best to keep her family together as they settle into their sod home, but when a handsome neighbor catches her eye, she fights against the urge to seek what little pleasures are available on the desolate plains. The children, Marta, Mary, and John, initially regard the brutal plains as a lively playground but slowly begin to realize that life is no longer fun and games. Through births, deaths, sicknesses, and windfalls, the Efkens stay together—sometimes for better, sometimes for worse—as they struggle to claim their piece of the American Dream.

Here's an example of a saga blurb filtered through one character's POV (notice how this tactic makes the book feel a bit "smaller," confined to John's experiences):

> *Across The Line* tells the interwoven stories of the Efkens, an 1860s family of immigrants who have fallen on hard times and decide to try their luck in the harsh prairies of the Nebraska frontier. The family's patriarch, John, struggles with the sense that he has failed his family, leading him to change from a warmhearted father into a domineering

and fearful tyrant. John fears that his perpetually pregnant wife, Emily, might be having an affair, and he struggles with the warring urges to see her happy and to see her remain *his*. His children, Marta, Mary, and John, initially regard the brutal plains as a lively playground, but slowly John watches as their spirits flag and their prospects grow increasingly dim. Through births, deaths, sicknesses, and windfalls, the Efkens stay together—sometimes for better, sometimes for worse—as they struggle to claim their piece of the American Dream.

ENSEMBLE CAST BOOKS do not have one main character; instead the characters, combined, function (for summarizing purposes) as if the whole group is a single character. The main climax is faced by the *group*, whether it's learning how to get along or trying to take down an evil dictator. Explore the common themes that bring your characters together: Why did you write these particular characters together in one story? A good strategy for organizing your book blurb is to offer a few words about each character's personality and main conflict, then summarize the rest of the story as if the group itself is a single character facing a single conflict.

Here's an example of an ensemble cast blurb:

The Light In Venice tells the story of three very different women who journey together to Venice on a work trip but discover surprising truths about their own inner lives. Millie is a take-no-prisoners career woman intent on climbing the corporate ladder at her advertising firm, but she's got a secret: She hates to be alone. In case the men of Italy aren't company enough, she decides to bring along her friend Alice. Alice, a stay-at-home mom, is dragged to Italy by Millie and is fearful of leaving her children—only to discover that time away from her kids might be just what she needs to be a better mom. Cosima, Millie's young and pliable assistant, is as driven as Millie when it comes to hard work—but Italy's lessons of food and wine teach her that there's more to life than pleasing the boss. Together, the three women must face the joys and challenges of overseas travel, but what they go home with is more than just a handful of souvenirs; it's a new way of life.

LITERARY NOVELS tend to resist traditional summaries—and that makes it especially hard to offer a summary. In literary novels, the focus is sometimes on theme, experience, relationships, philosophies, and style more so than on plot.

Here's an example of a literary novel blurb:

Good Love is a story told backward: When we meet the Wilsons, they are nothing more than an article in the local newspaper, a typical husband-wife murder-suicide case in a small Midwest town. No one quite knows what happened: Who shot who? And why?

In the beginning, Ralph and Rosemary Wilson are idealistic young lovers with dreams of a nice house, a quiet family, and a few good friends. But both husband and wife are keeping secrets: Ralph had been abused as a child, and Rosemary was not the innocent she pretended to be on her wedding night. And yet, for the most part, the two seem happy enough.

But as their fifty-year marriage comes to a close, the Wilsons' days of neighborhood picnics and quiet evenings spent watching TV give way to an increasingly twisted relationship. The past that never bothered them before becomes a point of contention. *Good Love* explores what happens when good love goes bad. As the Wilsons hang on to their pre-marriage secrets, they become complacent in their relationship, until lethargy and indifference finally breed the violence that will drive them toward their surprising fate.

Choose The Right Point Of View For Your Query Letter

It might seem that the point of view (POV) in a query letter would be straightforward: the letter is written from the viewpoint of the author, and the book blurb (or summary) is written like the copy on the back jacket of a book. But it's not always that simple.

Point Of View In Query Letters For Nonfiction

If you've written a memoir from the first-person point of view, the most common approach to take in your query letter summary is to write in first person as well. This makes sense: Your memoir is *your* story. Readers want to hear from *you*—not a version of you that's filtered through an awkward third-person narrator. The first-person POV is intimate, direct, and transparent.

However, we've read some very good memoir summaries written in the third person; there's no rule against taking that approach. Some writers decide to compose their entire memoir in third person. In this case, a third-person summary in a query letter would make sense.

If you're writing how-to, self-help, history, biography, etc., you should stay with first-person POV: With these kinds of nonfiction, your author platform (who you are as a writer) matters. So write your book summary as if you're telling a good friend about how amazing/life-changing/surprising your book is.

Point Of View In Query Letters For Novels

Novelists have a trickier time when it comes to point of view. Your overall letter is from your own point of view. But your book blurb (summary) has an implied narrator. Without getting too technical, let's say that your book blurb narrator has to usher readers into the minds (and lives) of the characters, in part through point of view.

Most people choose third-person omniscient for the book blurb/summary part of their letter, then switch back to first person for the rest of their letter. Rarely do second- or first-person summaries "work" in query letters, except in that very rare circumstance when a book's narrator has a strong voice. Even then, that strategy is dicey. Not impossible, but dicey.

Point Of View: Advanced Techniques For Storytellers

As previously noted, most people choose the POV of their main character (or the character who stands to lose or change the most) for their query blurb. If you've only got one main character, then you've got it easy: Filter the action through the eyes of your MC. By not "head hopping" in your query, you allow the reader to sink more deeply into the POV of one character, which creates a firmer emotional connection between character and reader than if you were to jump around.

Here's an example of a query letter blurb with one POV:

> Joe Brown's life is perfect: He's got a smoking hot wife, a quarterback son, and a purebred dog that doesn't even bark at strangers. And yet he's plagued by nightmares, vivid and disconcerting dreams of biological experiments that he can't quite remember—until one day, he does. And he realizes that his wife, his kid, and even his dog are nothing more than decoys hired by his former employer, Thorn Labs. In fact, Joe Brown isn't even his real name.
>
> Now, the only person who believes him is the annoying thirteen-year-old boy next door who happens to have a love of spy gear. But the more Joe learns about his former self, the less he likes him. And it's hard to give up the American Dream—even if it's a false one. He loves his wife. He loves his son. Is he willing to give them up in the name of truth, or should he just go on living the lie?

As you can see, the entire blurb above focuses on Joe. But for some book genres and situations, confining your query blurb to a single POV just won't work. In certain genres like romance, two or more POVs is typical and even expected.

Here's a book blurb with a deliberate POV change demarcated by a paragraph break:

> Joe Brown's life is perfect: He's got a smoking hot wife, a quarterback son, and a purebred dog that doesn't even bark at strangers. And yet he's plagued by nightmares, vivid and disconcerting dreams of biological experiments that he can't quite remember—until one day, he does. And he realizes that his wife, his son, and even his dog are nothing more than decoys hired by his

former employer, Thorn Labs. In fact, Joe Brown isn't even his real name.

Meanwhile, his "wife," Ellie Brown, has a problem: If her husband discovers the truth about his former identity as a lead scientist in the study of memory manipulation, her own child will be killed. But as the old Joe begins to disappear and the real Joe reemerges, Ellie can't help her growing feelings for her false husband. With the government becoming suspicious that "the subject" is catching on, Ellie begins to wonder if there's more to her marriage than she'd ever thought possible—but she won't find out unless she can keep her husband and child alive.

Here, the POV change is obvious, in part because of the paragraph break that separates one POV from the other. But sometimes POV shifts are not so clear.

POV changes can be subtle. In fact, many new writers will shift POV in a query letter book blurb without quite realizing they're doing it. The shift is often no more than a phrase or a sentence long—but it is a shift in perspective. If not done carefully, shifting POV can disrupt the flow of the query blurb.

Let's look at an example of a query blurb with sneaky POV shifts.

Here, multiple secondary characters chime in with their POV on the main action, and as a result, this blurb feels a bit weak:

> When Julie "Sass" Krough opens the doors of her bar one summer evening, she expects a typical night filled with bikers, truckers, and women looking for trouble. What she doesn't expect is a full-scale sting operation going down on her dance floor that ends with her and her bartender, Joan, being thrown in jail for a drug-trafficking crime they definitely didn't commit. Joan believes that someone wants to cause problems for Julie, and she decides to do a little digging on behalf of her friend.
>
> [Editorial note: Why use Joan as the lens for this information, when Julie is the person with the most to lose? Better to show the action through Julie's eyes.]
>
> The path leads to Dylan, an ex-marine and the former owner of Julie's bar. Dylan has always been jealous of Julie because of her success with the bar, believing that she shortchanged him during their negotiations. Julie can't believe Dylan would do anything to harm

her; in fact, she sometimes has wondered if they might have chemistry. Joan convinces Julie not to trust him, but Dylan insists that Joan is playing them both because she wants the bar for herself. Now, with angry drug-traffickers looking for answers, Julie has to decide who to trust—and the wrong decision won't just mean the loss of the bar: She could lose her life.

This book blurb starts out clearly in Julie's POV, but we lose the ability to sympathize with her because the critical information about the conflict isn't provided from Julie's viewpoint. Instead, we get bits of information through secondary characters, and the blurb loses emotional momentum.

You might ask: *But isn't this blurb simply an example of omniscient point of view?* And yes, it is. But since elements of the action are filtered through the eyes of various secondary characters instead of the primary character, this is considered a shift in POV. The point is not to shift POVs if you don't absolutely need to—doing so breaks the flow of your summary. You should pay as much attention to POV in your query as in your book itself. Summarize your story through the eyes of the character(s) who stand to lose/change the most.

Follow Your Instincts

Not all books will accommodate a query letter blurb that focuses primarily on one or two POVs. Sometimes POVs must jump around. Villains need their moment in the sun. Secondary characters sometimes offer key insight into elements that the main character can't comprehend. In situations where the information must come through a secondary character, remember to keep the tension high for your main character, and your point of view choice will be fine.

The Most Common POV Mistakes In Query Letters

In a good query summary, the reader is so engrossed in the story that he or she almost forgets he/she is reading. A good query pulls the reader into the story—it doesn't remind them that they are reading.

In the (very bad) novel blurb below, we'll boldface the phrases that are unnecessarily self-referential, intrusive, or reflexive. In a revision, these phrases should be eliminated.

> **The book opens** when we meet Julie Kern: She's trying to kick a half-drunk, ex-cop biker, Malcolm Black, out of her bar, and the fireworks fly. Soon, **this** relationship [note: as opposed to *their* relationship] eventually brings them both to the realization that if they want to clean up neighborhood crime, they've got to join forces. **In the end,** the two must confront a dangerous drug lord to reclaim their turf, **leaving readers with a feeling of breathlessness and surprise.**

Here's the same text without the self-referential phrases:

> When tough-as-nails bar owner Julie Kern tries to kick a half-drunk, ex-cop biker named Malcolm Black out of her bar one night, the fireworks fly. But it isn't long before she realizes that she and Malcolm have something in common: They both want to clean up neighborhood crime, and they're better off working as a team than working alone. Their struggle to rid their street of drug traffic leads them to a dangerous dealer who wants them off his turf. Julie's willing to trust Malcolm with her life. But as their risky plan to scare away the drug cartel brings them closer together, she realizes there's something more at stake than her safety: her heart.

What Your Book Blurb Must Do If You Want To Get An Agent

Do you know how to spot the difference between a good query letter and a fantastic query letter? This is going to sound trite, but the answer is: *Ask your heart.*

That's right—the single most important thing that your query letter can do if you want to get a literary agent's attention is create an emotional experience for the reader. You've got to make your reader feel. You've got to give him or her a reason to become invested in your story.

For that reason, telling the bare facts of "what happens in the story" is not going to get your book a lot of attention. The book publishing industry is competitive. And when a literary agent is faced with two similar stories—one that is presented as a series of facts and one that offers an emotional experience—you can bet the literary agent is going to ask to see the book that gives him or her goose bumps.

So How Is A Writer Supposed To Create An Emotional Experience In A Query Letter Book Blurb?

Step One: Win us with your character. Unless we really care about your main character, it's hard to become invested in the story. You don't need an excessive amount of detail to demonstrate who your character is: A few precise descriptions that embody personality, strengths, and weaknesses should do the job. Bonus points if those descriptions hint at your character's fatal flaw.

Step Two: Now that we care about the character, show us what that person has to lose. It's human nature to have a big emotional response when a loved one faces a tough challenge. The same goes for great characters: We care about them because of their vulnerability. So show us just how much is at risk.

Step Three: Choose the right words. As a writer, words are your medium. By choosing evocative words over dull words—and by choosing exciting phrases over flat ones—you can create a deeper sense of emotionality.

> **EXAMPLE 1:** Our Hero hides in an underground bunker to escape terrorists. Townspeople begin flocking to the hideout, and this attracts attention and makes Our Hero the target of the terrorists, who have found out where he is. He retreats into an underground tunnel system to get away.

This whole scene should feel like an intense action sequence. And yet all of the emotion of the moment is buried under dull word choices and muddled sentences. So let's try again, except with a more emotional approach.

> **EXAMPLE 2:** To escape the terrorists, Our Hero hides out in an earthen bunker—but his location is compromised when the people of Smithtown come banging on the hideout door, seeking safety for themselves and their loved ones. Now Our Hero's cover is blown—the terrorists know where he is. There's no choice but to brave the dangerous underground tunnel system that extends out of the bunker. But with the enemy on to him, will he get out alive?

The first example is a rote description of the action; the second pulls us into the action to experience it with him. We *feel* his fear.

The Bottom Line: You've Got To Make Readers Care

A great query letter is not just a summary; it is an emotional experience that makes the reader want to know more. Literary agents may read dozens of query letters a day that don't make their hearts race—but if your query letter makes them care about your sympathetic characters by exposing vulnerabilities, emphasizing risk, and choosing evocative words, then you might just have a winner.

5 Essential Strategies For A More Emotionally Compelling Query

1. Show, don't tell. You've heard this advice before in your creative writing workshops. But did you know it applies to your query letter too? Sure, a query letter synopsis requires *lots* of telling and summary, but when possible, add in concrete details. Instead of "After hearing her dog died, Lara was sad," try "After hearing her dog died, Lara drowned her sorrows in a pint of ice cream." Just be sure not to overdo it.

2. The specific always trumps the general. Rather than saying "Defeated once again, Robert went home," try "Defeated again, Robert skulked back to his basement apartment." Or, rather than saying your character wore magical shoes, say she wore ruby slippers (or steampunk-style hovercraft Keds).

3. Set the mood. Mood is a key ingredient we see missing from many query letters. Sure, you can tell a story, but are you using language to evoke a certain mood—and all the emotions that go with that mood? Investigate your own choice of adjectives and adverbs (if you're using any) and see if they're doing a good job of evoking the right tone. Think of the difference between *sad* and *forlorn*. Between *ebullient* and *glad*. What mood are you evoking with your word choices?

4. Use your setting. Before you launch into your story, consider taking a moment to illuminate your story's setting. Why? Storytelling is all about the five senses, and when you offer strong, compelling descriptions, you give your reader something concrete to latch on to and become immersed in.

5. Focus on high stakes. Now that you've got the tools to hook your reader with emotion, it's time to focus on the story itself. Think of your protagonist. What's the worst thing that will happen if he/she doesn't succeed? That's what's going to make your reader feel an emotional investment in your character. You don't want to give away your ending in your query letter (save that for your synopsis), but you do want to hint that it will be meaningful and full of momentum.

6 Sample Query Letters For Novels And Memoirs That Worked

A successful query is one that stimulates a literary agent to request more materials: sample pages, a synopsis, or the complete manuscript. The query letters we include in this section were all successfully used by Writer's Relief clients who were generous enough to allow us to publish their letters in order to help you write yours. We've removed contact information and changed certain elements by client request.

We hope you'll enjoy!

Sample Query (Fiction)

This query letter for a literary/upmarket novel features lively language, great characters, a unique angle, and a well-defined plot arc with plenty of room for character growth. We're thrilled with our collaboration with this author, who gave us great raw material to start with and who contributed colorful language and lots of personality. Is it any wonder agents were excited about this book?

Dear Agent:

Please consider my literary novel, *The Ballad of Mr. Joe*, for representation. It's the tale of a renegade, rock-and-roll, world-renowned antique Islamic carpet expert and his train wreck of a life.

Joe Krooney looks like an aging rock star; he acts like one too, spewing profanity and screwing women at every stop on his world tours. But Mr. Joe doesn't tour with a band; he's really the Indiana Jones of rugs, on the hunt for ultra-rare textiles.

After authenticating a fake carpet for a major Los Angeles museum—destroying the career of his former lover and mother of his child in the process—Joe finds himself broke, alone, and disgraced. "Borrowing" his brother's credit card, Joe books a first-class crossing to England on the *Queen Mary 2* to rock it out one last time before jumping overboard.

On the ship he meets the Browns, a troubled young couple, and forms an unlikely bond with their eight-year-old son. For his last (and maybe only) good deed, Joe decides to help the couple's foundering marriage and save the boy from a childhood like his own. When they discover Joe's plan to commit suicide, they intervene and invite Joe on their vacation. He takes the family on a high-speed adventure through the streets of Paris, revisiting former conquests and running into real rock stars. A transformative experience, the journey forces Joe to take a hard look at his past. How far is he willing to go to repair the collateral damage from his life? Can he find the courage to open his heart to the woman and child he abandoned years earlier? More importantly: Will they let him?

I graduated with a B.A. in English from the University of Pennsylvania, where I was a writer for *The Daily Pennsylvanian*. A member of the Actors Studio, I've worked extensively in theater, film, and television.

Chock-full of sex, drugs, and rock-and-roll, *The Ballad of Mr. Joe* is complete at 100,000 words. Thank you for reading.

Sincerely,

Writer's Relief Client

Sample Query (Fiction)

This client's letter format is traditional, leading with a log line-esque summary, then offering the book blurb and author bio. Note: The intro line is a little clever, but it's not over the top. First, it suggests the book genre in a traditional way. But then the author has a little fun with the description, hinting at elements that are surprising and funny. If the book purports to have a comic slant, the query letter must as well. And the author strikes the right tone from the get-go.

Dear Agent:

Please consider my novel, *The Guardian of Detritus*, for representation. You might say it's an 84,000-word comic thriller. I'd like to say it's a "coming-of-old-age," witty, noirish, action-packed mystery set in the exotic metropolis of Detroit.

Will Harkanen is a might-have-been rock star working in corporate PR who finds himself on the wrong side of middle age and on the brink of divorce. But when Will happens upon the obituary of an old friend, he immediately and enthusiastically quits his job. Not sure if he's having a breakdown or breakthrough, Will decides that it's time to pursue the dreams of his youth.

Finally free of the corporate grind, Will heads to Detroit for the funeral of his former friend, where he tries to reconcile with former band members and an ex-lover. Soon he discovers that a master recording of the band's second album—supposedly destroyed years ago—may have resurfaced. Not a big deal—except the tape just might be related to his friend's increasingly suspicious death.

While dodging the mayhem of a big movie set and scrambling through the back alleys of Detroit, Will begins to unravel the tangled mess of blackmail, bribery, and corruption that surrounds his friend's death. And with his youthful dreams suddenly starting to come true as he investigates, Will soon realizes that he should have been careful what he wished for.

I am an award-winning speech writer whose clients have included the senior executives of two of the top five biggest companies in the world, six chairmen of the board, a famous/infamous Detroit politician, and a member of British Parliament. My book, *Speech Right: How to Write a Great Speech*, was published by Aventine Press in 2010 and is used in numerous college courses.

Thanks for taking a look at my manuscript. I look forward to hearing from you.

Sincerely,

Chuck Snearly
www.speechright.com

Sample Query (Fiction)

For this client, we opted to split the writer's extensive and impressive bio into two sections. Featuring strong credits in the beginning of a letter can sometimes help to put the reader in a positive and receptive state of mind even before the book itself is described. But since the agent will be itching to read about the story itself, we didn't want *too* much emphasis on background right up in front. For that reason, we chose to lead with a few fabulous credits to drum up some early excitement, then include the book blurb, then feature the rest of the writer's credits to really drive her talent home. This one's a winner!

Dear Agent:

I am a graduate of the Iowa Writers' Workshop, where I received my MFA in fiction writing. Please consider my coming-of-age novel, *The Criminal Gene*. "The Criminal Gene," the story on which the novel is based, was nominated for *Best American Mystery Stories* after appearing in the *Apalachee Review*. "McTheft," a short story excerpted from the novel, is forthcoming in *Shark Reef*.

The Criminal Gene: When Nina Burd, a teenage shoplifter obsessed with family history, gets caught stealing in Iowa and is sent to live in suburban New York with two wealthy great-aunts she's never met, she discovers that she comes from a long line of female criminals. Learning that her snooty relatives jimmy cars for a living is only the first shock for Nina. Her grandmother, Kitty, a talented jewel thief who died under mysterious circumstances, appears as a ghost and begs Nina to find the diary that Kitty hid in parts throughout the house. As Nina explores her criminal gifts, with disastrous consequences, she uncovers long-buried secrets that threaten the family's very core.

My short fiction has also appeared in *The Florida Review, Willow Review, Southern Indiana Review, Grey Sparrow, Conte, North Dakota Quarterly, Portland Review, Washington Square, Southern Humanities Review, Forge, PMS, Amarillo Bay, Pearl, Main Street Rag,* and in other journals. The novel takes place in Katonah, New York, my hometown. My knowledge of auto theft came about as a teenager watching my boyfriend (now husband) "borrow" cars from friends. And, like several of my characters, I'm a fallen debutante.

The novel is complete at 98,000 words. Thank you for considering my work.

Sincerely,

Nancy Scott Hanway

Sample Query (Fiction)

Here's another client with a wonderful background. Are you sensing a pattern here? Not all of our clients have established reputations as writers, but those who do have some publications credits tend to receive a bit more agent attention for their queries. Writer's Relief often helps our clients get stories, poems, essays, and excerpts published in literary journals before querying agents with a book.

In this letter, we collaborated with the client to convey her passion for her unique subject matter. Can you feel how much she loves this story (without coming off in any way as arrogant)? Agents found it to be contagious!

Dear Agent:

I am submitting my 81,000-word historical novel, *The Silver Baron's Wife*, inspired by the true story of early feminist and mystic "Baby Doe" Tabor.

My writing has appeared in *Prairie Schooner, Virginia Quarterly Review, New York Quarterly, Puerto del Sol, Confrontation,* and many other journals and anthologies. I'm also the publisher of the literary journal *Tiferet*. My story collection, *Sympathetic People*, was published by Serving House Books in December 2013. My poetry chapbook, *Sometimes You Sense the Difference*, was published by Finishing Line Press in 2012. I've received four Pushcart nominations, a fellowship from Johns Hopkins University Writing Seminars, a scholarship from Bread Loaf Writers' Conference, a finalist place in the Iowa Fiction Awards, an honorable mention in Allen Ginsberg Poetry Awards, the PEN New England Discovery Award for my novel *Fortune*, and more.

The Silver Baron's Wife is the incredible account of an intrepid and fascinating figure in American history, and I'm so excited to bring her story to light. In 1866, twelve-year-old Lizzie McCourt watches as her father's Wisconsin tailoring business goes up in flames. Ten years later, eager for respectability and social standing, she marries the mayor's son, Harvey Doe, and follows him to Colorado.

When Harvey proves a disappointment as both husband and provider, Lizzie herself goes down into the mines, drawn by their mystery and promise. After divorcing her unfaithful husband, she catches the eye of Horace Tabor, a silver baron thirty years her senior and one of the wealthiest men in America. Amid a great scandal, Horace leaves his wife and son to marry Lizzie in an extravagant ceremony attended by some of the nation's most illustrious men.

Horace and Lizzie build a sumptuous villa in Denver, but the Gilded Age elite turn a cold shoulder.

With the repeal of the Sherman Silver Purchase Act in 1893, Horace's fortune is eventually lost. But Lizzie does not abandon her husband; she stays at his side until his death once more sets her adrift. She goes back to the mines in her final search for riches, happiness, and her place in the world.

I hope you are intrigued by Lizzie's story, which I feel mirrors the spiritual paths of many modern-day women. The full manuscript is available upon request.

Sincerely,

Donna Baier Stein
www.donnabaierstein.com

Sample Query (Memoir)

Here we have a query letter for a memoir that immediately draws the reader in by making the writer's emotional viewpoint instantly relatable. The mood is set for her experiences in Lithuania using dramatic, tension-filled description of the events that transpired. In a memoir, how the story ends may not be unknown—but the path to get there can be compelling and still have cliffhanger elements.

Dear Agent:

Thank you for considering my completed 100,000-word memoir, *Making Bullets: Take One California Girl. Add a Lithuanian Revolution. Stir.*

As the American-born daughter of Lithuanian WWII refugees, my parents always said it was my duty to preserve their culture. Growing up, I resented being torn between being American and being Lithuanian; I wanted to be a typical American girl who went to the mall and the beach with her friends—not a girl who learned folk dancing and an archaic language.

But when Gorbachev took power in the USSR and Lithuanians began a revolution for independence, I realized I wanted to learn more about the heritage I had shunned. In 1991, at the age of 25, I arrived in Lithuania two days after the Soviet military attempted a violent coup against the Lithuanian government.

As tensions rose, I was not prepared for the wartime conditions: maneuvering Soviet bureaucracy and martial law, buying supplies from Gypsies and toilet paper on the black market, and the constant Soviet military aggression against the Lithuanian people. By chance, I found myself working as a press spokesperson at the Lithuanian Parliament.

When Gorbachev was taken hostage, initiating the August 1991 Coup, Soviet tanks surrounded the Lithuanian Parliament building. Barricaded inside, my coworkers and I prepared to make a final stand for freedom with nothing more than Molotov cocktails and antiquated hunting rifles. As the tanks adjusted their barrels and lined up their shots, I finally began to understand what being born a Lithuanian-American—with all of my American freedoms and my Lithuanian traditions—really meant.

I was awarded the Lithuanian State Honor Commemorative Medal of January 13 for my efforts during the fight for independence. I am now a master's candidate for humanities with an emphasis in cultural studies. I guest lecture at schools and social groups about the Baltic revolutions and the Soviet collapse and am a member of the Association for the Advancement of Baltic Studies. I am also a featured guest blogger on LTUworld.com, a Lithuanian news and social platform. In my spare time, I enjoy volunteering at the Los Angeles Midnight Mission homeless shelter and the Daughters of Lithuania charity. I'm also an avid mountain climber and recently trekked up to the Everest Base Camp.

I look forward to hearing your thoughts about my memoir. I hope my story—and the story of a fight for identity and independence—interests you. Thank you for considering my work.

Sincerely,

Daiva Venckus
www.daivavenckus.com

Sample Query (Memoir)

This memoir shows the success the author has had with excerpts from her memoir. Again, being able to prove that there is an interest in and a market for your writing is an important plus when trying to capture a literary agent's attention.

Dear Agent:

Please consider my 55,400-word memoir, *Why Is God In Daddy's Slippers?* for representation.

The memoir is set in a lower-middle-class area in Cambridge in the 1960s where, as a child, I am haunted by the tensions and secrets of my Irish and Italian family. My continual and humorous misunderstandings of Catholic beliefs, urban folklore, and gender and ethnic stereotypes help me construct bizarre fantasies that overshadow my real childhood world.

Written from a child's perspective, I perform exorcisms, keep pets out of purgatory, discover the "holy" in holy water, find God in my father's smelly slippers, and barely escape a visitation by the Virgin Mary. Unlike conventional treatments of Catholicism that depict religion as solely a source of childhood anxiety, the book also illustrates how the magic nature of religion enabled me to temporarily resolve the anxieties of daily life. As I approached puberty, the females in my life, from my friends, to my aunts, to the Virgin Mary, intervene—sometimes hilariously, sometimes tragically—as I continually am made to rethink what it is like to be a modern young woman.

I am a professor of literature and pedagogy at Purchase College, SUNY. Early versions of some chapters have appeared in *Calyx, Compass Rose, The Dirty Goat, Fugue, Italian Americana, Lullwater Review, North Atlantic Review, Northwest Review, Pig Iron Press, PoemMemoirStory, The Rambler, REAL, A River and Sound Review, Rock & Sling, The South Carolina Review, Stringtown, Westview, Willow Review, Witness,* and *Zone 3*. A portion of one chapter, "I Always Felt Like I Was on Pretty Good Terms with the Virgin Mary Even Though I Didn't Get Pregnant in High School," won first prize in the 2009 *Tiny Lights* creative nonfiction contest and was performed in Petaluma, CA, in 2012. I'm negotiating with an NYC theater company to do readings of other pieces. My book *The Culture of Reading and the Teaching of English* (Manchester UP and NCTE, 1994) won the Modern Language Association's Mina P. Shaughnessy Prize for an outstanding work on the teaching of language and literature. Other academic books include *Teaching*

Italian American Literature, Film, and Popular Culture and *Approaches to Teaching James Joyce's* Ulysses.

I'd be happy to send you the complete manuscript for your review. Thank you for your time.

Sincerely,

Kathleen McCormick
www.kathleenzmccormick.com

Element #4: Your Author Bio: Make A Great Impression!

Your bio is a short paragraph about you, and writing a good professional bio is no easy task. First, you have to determine your most pertinent credentials. Then, you have to decide on the most flattering way to present them. Some writers find it easy to write an author bio. But the majority of writers struggle with it, especially when they're first starting out as an author.

Your author bio offers agents a glimpse into who you are, so it's important that you include the right information.

Your Author Bio Checklist

Composing a professional writing bio for a query letter can be challenging, whether you're a new writer with no publication credits, a mid-level writer with significant publications, or a professional writer. Agents sometimes look to a writer's publication history to help them make a decision about a submission.

The author bio in your query letter should be good—and while this book stresses the importance of having strong publication credits, we want to reiterate that it's not unheard of for a writer with no experience to gain national attention. Just be sure that the author bio in your query letter is professional, succinct, accurate, and helpful.

Refer To This Checklist When You're Writing Your Author Bio

Length Of Your Author Bio

- DO keep it short. Your professional writing bio should be no more than one paragraph—two at the very most.

- DON'T attach your résumé, CV, or other professional documents unless they are specifically requested. Literary agents won't read them; they might skim them (if you're lucky). And if you don't prominently emphasize what is most important in your author bio, your best publishing credits may be overlooked. Agents don't want to scroll or flip through multiple pages to find your best credentials.

Your Creative Writing Publication Credits

- DO put your best writing credits first, where they'll get noticed. But how do you know which are best? We'll explain more in an upcoming section.

- DON'T include publishing credits that will peg you as an amateur, like disreputable poetry contests or shady Who's Who listings. Again, more specifics will follow.

- DO stick to the facts. Don't overinflate or falsify.

- DO always include the **name of the publisher** and **publication date** if you are listing a book in your bio. Example: *The Book I Wrote* (AnyName Publishers, 2010). The book title alone is not enough for industry professionals, and failing to include this key information could indicate that you don't yet know the etiquette.
- DO include any accolades or quotes from well-known reviewers, especially for self-published books.

Your Personality And Your Professional Writing Bio

- DON'T give details about your particular writing philosophies; sorry, but agents don't want to hear about your creative process in your bio. Save it for your interviews when you're famous.

- DO consider including some personal information if it's appropriate to your submission or if it might set you apart. We'll go into detail in a later section.

- DO be consistent. You can write your bio in first person or third (though first is more common). Whichever you choose, stick with it.

What To Do If You Have No Publishing Credits In Your Bio

Don't panic; literary agents know that everyone has to start somewhere—even you. There's no need to state in your letters that you're unpublished—you don't need to "apologize" for being new. Just use our tips to write a bio that succinctly gives readers a glimpse into your commitment to your craft.

At Writer's Relief, we know there's no substitute for patience when it comes to getting your work published. But if you want to build up your writing credentials quickly, **here are some smart ways to improve your professional writing bio AND your writing skills.**

Develop a good submission strategy. When you're carefully researching, targeting markets, and sending work out into the world, you're creating opportunities for yourself. When you're not sending out your writing or if you're submitting haphazardly, you're not making opportunities for yourself. So develop a good submission strategy that gets your work out there!

Join a well-known writing organization. Are you writing romance? Join Romance Writers of America. Are you creating high-end literary works? Check out the Association of Writing Programs. You will probably need to pay some fees to join these organizations, but the benefits are endless. First, you'll get to put their well-known name on your query letter. Second, you'll get access to lots of great resources and benefit from great networking opportunities. And third, you'll show literary agents that you're committed to and serious about your writing—whether you've published anything or not!

Join a little-known writing organization. Writers all over the country are conducting workshops, and they may be meeting in your area. Including "I attend a weekly writing workshop meeting" in your query letter shows that you're resourceful and diligent. Not only that, your writing technique will benefit greatly, and you may meet other like-minded writers and make friends. Often these types of meetings are free. Just be sure to take all necessary precautions to stay safe. HINT: Find lists of reputable writers organizations on our website: www.writersrelief.com/writers-associations-organizations.

Volunteer. By volunteering for the spring cleanup at your local library—or by devoting your time to other worthy literary endeavors—you demonstrate that you care deeply about the written word. Agents like to see writers who are dedicated to their craft beyond their own personal gain.

Take classes. Even if you don't have many (or any) publishing credentials, taking a class establishes your commitment to being a professional writer. It will help your technique and your reputation. Being able to state in your query letter that you took a class at the University of XYZ may strike a chord with agents.

Go to a writing conference. If your budget permits, attend a writing conference. Not only will you learn and network, but you'll also be able to mention in your bio that you attended the conference. A writing conference is like an awards show after-party—everyone who's anyone will be there. If an agent recognizes the name of the conference (maybe he or she attended, or perhaps knows a colleague who did), that may tip the scales in your favor.

Please note: It goes without saying that you should only use these strategies if you can implement them with honesty and true dedication to your craft. Don't make things up just to pad your credentials and appear more established. Plus, taking the aforementioned steps won't just build up your bio; it will build your abilities and reputation as a writer.

There's no substitute for good old-fashioned publication credits at literary journals, independent presses, and large publishing houses. But while you're working to build up your publication credits, it's our opinion that demonstrating an authentic commitment to craft and to the writing community can work in your favor.

Example Of A Bio For A Writer Who Has No Publishing Credits Yet

Here's an example of a bio from a writer who hasn't actually published anything yet but is on his/her way:

> *I work as a grassroots coordinator for a local environmental organization, and when I'm not at work, I'm writing or reading or working on my craft. I've taken classes at the XYZ Studio in New York, and I've also personally studied with Famous Author Name. Last year I attended the Name of Writers Group conference. I regularly volunteer at my local library as a reader for one-on-one sessions with disadvantaged kids.*

See? Even though this writer has no publishing credits yet, he/she has laid the foundation for future success. Agents and editors love to discover undiscovered talent. Plus, this writer seems nice—generous and passionate. When you're asking another professional to work with you, "nice" goes a long way.

The Publishing Credits Shuffle

At some point, writers who are dedicated and diligent encounter a fantastic problem: What is the best way to organize multiple publication credits in a professional writing bio?

While each writer may make his or her own decisions based on personal preferences and goals, we can offer some answers to common questions.

Should every publishing credit be included?
At Writer's Relief, we recommend that our clients keep their list of accomplishments and publications to one brief bio paragraph. This means that if your work has appeared in thirty literary journals, it may be a good idea to include only the highest-ranked journals on your list.

What is the best order for publishing credits?
There are two schools of thought: You can order your list of published works in alphabetical order; or you can list them by reputation (so your most prestigious credentials come first). You can also combine the two methods—leading off with *The New Yorker*, and then moving on to list other publications in alphabetical order.

There's really no wrong answer here; it's a personal choice. Some writers prefer the orderly and organized approach to listing credits. Others like their most important credits listed first.

Does it help to list "smaller" publishing credentials in a query letter?
While some writers opt to leave "smaller" publishing credits out of their query letters, we recommend that writers consider the ramifications carefully before making such omissions.

Once you've had your work published in highly significant journals or with major publishers, then you might consider leaving off some of those smaller credits. However, remember that listing your many publishing credits—and the range of journals/magazines/etc. that you've been published in—demonstrates that you are more than just a hobbyist. If a credit is reputable, it certainly won't hurt you. It could even help you—but not if you leave it out.

What about student publications?
Most of the time, listing publication credits that you got through a very small, student-run, local magazine while you were in high school or college isn't going to help your cause too much. And it could make you look like you're "reaching."

That said, some colleges have phenomenal literary journals with massive reputations, so if you were published in one of those, you should definitely consider including it in your bio.

Which Kinds Of Publishing Credits Are Best?

Which of your writing bio credits have the most weight, and which are less substantial? Sometimes it's hard to tell.

There is a certain hierarchy in terms of which credits impress and which are so-so. If you're trying to determine the best way to organize your author bio, the list below will help. We've ordered it so the "best" kinds of writing credits appear first.

CAVEAT: There are nuances that are not reflected in our list (because each writer's situation is different). Also, keep in mind that this list will shift a little depending on what genre you're publishing in (for example, few poets publish collections with major publishing houses, so not having such a credit isn't unusual).

Bio Credits: From Gold, To Silver, To Bronze, To Tinfoil

Bestsellerhood. If you're a *New York Times* best seller, that should probably go first. No need to be modest! If you worked hard enough to get there, go ahead and boast!

Book publications with a major publisher. If you're with a big, name-brand publishing house, that's pretty high on the list of things that will impress literary agents.

Publications with a major indie press. Independent publishing houses are taken seriously (some more than others, of course).

Impressive awards. Even if you don't win, there are some awards that are cool just to be nominated for (we're looking at you, *Pushcart Prize* nominees!). It's a good idea to lead with these accolades.

Publication in highly regarded literary journals. *Ploughshares*, *The New York Times*, even *Vogue* and *Esquire*... These are some magazines that are the crème de la crème. If you're not alphabetizing your list of credits, lead with those.

Publication in reputable venues. Solid, middle-of-the-road publications, whether online or in print, can be the bread and butter of a life's work.

Readings in well-known venues. Some writers are asked to read at places like Housing Works (a famed nonprofit bookstore in NYC where big names make regular appearances). And if you're in a particular genre, there are probably reading salons that are well-known in your niche.

Writing residencies. Most residencies (like Yaddo and Vermont Studio Center) are pretty competitive. So if you're selected to participate in a reputable residency, be sure to note it in your bio.

Writing-related careers. Unless you're a senior editor at Random House, your career may reflect your talent as a writer, but it probably isn't as impressive as having actual publication credits and awards. You'll have to use your judgment on this one, as every career is different.

Blogging. Mention your blog to entice readers, to demonstrate that you have a strong author platform, and to show that you're market savvy. (Agents love bloggers!) And if you have many readers, brag about them! If your blog is a big part of your author platform, your blog may float to the top of your list of credentials. But keep in mind that anyone can publish a blog. You'll have to decide if your blog has a big brag factor. Perhaps it does!

Publication in so-so venues. Everyone has to start somewhere! Your local literary journal may not have a huge following, but it counts!

Minor awards. There are some awards that aren't very well-known, and others that are not considered reputable. Legitimate writing contests include those for writers who are at the high end of the craft spectrum (these contests usually have impressive editors), and contests that are more suitable for beginners. Just be sure you're not boasting about winning a disreputable Who's Who award or a shady poetry contest. When in doubt, proceed with caution.

Professional writing groups. Listing the groups you're active in may help your cause, especially if those groups have national recognition (like Mystery Writers of America or Science Fiction and Fantasy Writers of America).

Professional writing conferences. If you've been given a full fellowship to Bread Loaf, that's seriously worth prioritizing. If you're going to a local writers conference that isn't really well-known, that information can still be helpful (to show you're serious), but that credit may not be quite as impressive as attending more celebrated conferences.

Self-publishing. Read more about the right way to share your self-publishing credentials in Part Eight: Special Considerations.

Readings in amateur venues. Have you been asked to read at a small coffee shop? Go, you! Are you a regular at the local open mike? That also might be worth mentioning.

Amateur writing groups. If you're meeting with neighbors to discuss poetry, that can show you're serious about your craft.

Other Variables

Depending on your goals and intentions, the following may be more (or less) important in your bio when you're making submissions.

Fake Writing Contests And Your Author Bio: Don't Be Fooled!

When you begin researching contests and publications for your submissions, watch for anything that looks too good to be true—it probably is!

You've seen the ads in the Sunday newspaper magazines—a mass-market appeal to submit your poem, get published, and win a huge prize.

There's no shortage of writing contests out there. And in most cases, the goals of these contests are legitimate: recognizing and honoring quality writing and beefing up membership or subscription bases at literary journals that depend on readers to keep publishing.

Unfortunately, there's no dearth of con artists in this world, and questionable competitions are everywhere, luring both "would-be" authors and established writers with seductive prizes and flattering appraisals of their work.

The warning signs of a disreputable writing contest:

Unusually large cash prizes. Especially when there's no entry fee. Where in the world do they find such financial backing? And *why*?

No prize money but a promise of "agent representation"—at a high price. Or an invitation to join "The International League of Super Amazing Poets"—for a pricey sum, of course.

Anthologies. Your poem was accepted, and the publisher is oozing high praise. Your stunning and highly acclaimed poem will be published in an anthology—and would you like to purchase said anthology for $49.95? How about your proud friends and family? For several hundred dollars, you and yours can each have a copy of your poem in published form…you know the sales pitch.

Conventions. Again, your poem has been "accepted" and is lavishly praised. You've even won a prize! But you have to attend a convention to accept this prize, and naturally, the registration fee is a few hundred dollars.

Unknown contest sponsor. The name may seem familiar, but it's a word or two away from the name of a legitimate poetry organization. Research the company on the Internet.

Contest sponsor is difficult to contact. Is there a phone number? A contact name? A dodgy website? Are your questions answered quickly, or is the response slow to come or evasive?

Advertisements in daily newspapers or magazines unrelated to the writing field. Legitimate organizations advertise contests in publications targeted for the writing community and do not spend money on mass-market publications.

Low standards. Each and every submission—from quality to awful—is accepted and lavishly praised.

Past winners are nowhere to be found. If it's impossible to find the work of past winners…you get the picture. However, if you are able to find the previous winners and their work is mediocre, then obviously the standards of the contest are so-so as well.

Short poems preferred (or required). The more writers the publishers can squeeze into one book, the more money they'll make when they try to sell copies to these writers (and families and friends).

If the warning bells clanging in your head aren't enough, do some research of your own. A Google search for "writing contest scams" will give you lists of the worst contests. If you're uncertain as to whether or not you have been published by a less-than-reputable "contest" or included in a dubious organization, leave that information out of your author bio.

Who's Who: The Truth About Special Directories

There are many "Who's Who" organizations that claim to create the definitive lists of professionals in a given industry. Some are legitimate, some are not, and some are just questionable.

We refer to all such organizations as "Who's Who" directories, since many of these companies use the term "Who's Who" to describe themselves. We are not referring to a specific company. Before you add a "Who's Who" credit to your bio in your query letter, be sure that you are not being misled by a money-making scheme.

Here's how they usually work:
A letter arrives, informing you that you are being considered for inclusion in a prestigious directory for writers, professionals, and executives. This is a reference publication containing brief biographical information for a particular group of people, supposedly people of note. As a writer, you are thrilled to be included among the nation's top professionals. What an honor! Just think of the networking possibilities! You can't wait to add your "Who's Who" credit to your author bio, since you're sure it will impress literary agents. The letter encourages you to fill out the enclosed application and return it—with special emphasis on this line: *There is no cost to be included in this fabulous directory.*

No cost!

Well, if there's no cost to you, it must be legitimate, right?

So you fill out the form and sit back, feeling good. A few weeks later you receive a congratulatory phone call from this esteemed directory, and the caller has quite a few questions for you, which you confidently answer. After this lengthy and flattering interview, you are feeling rather important and validated.

That's when they hit you with the hard sell: It's true that there's no cost to be listed in the directory. But if you want a copy of your interview and profile, you'll have to buy the hardcover book. And do you want a plaque to go with that? A personalized press release sent to the local paper featuring your big news? A chance to network with the other amazing people in the directory? Fork over your credit card number, please!

Then, when you fall over from shock at being asked to pay so much money, the friendly salesperson relents and offers you a super special deal—the same price offered to nonprofit charities and libraries—but this is a once-in-a-lifetime offer, and you'd better sign up quickly. How can you refuse?

How can you *not*?

If you've fallen for a "Who's Who" company scheme, don't feel bad. At some point, the lure of a "Who's Who" or a shady contest tempts everyone. Writers in particular must be careful not to fall prey to such scams.

Many "Who's Who" directories are not legitimate credits to add to your publishing bio; they work the same way as writing contest schemes.

If you list a "Who's Who" credit that literary agents do not recognize as legitimate, you'll appear naive. When a "Who's Who" organization calls you and asks for your money, do your research before you commit to anything. Then, if necessary, head for the hills. Ask that your name be taken off their list.

One final note: There are many legitimate and truly inspiring "Who's Who" directories out there. Just do your research before including any in your author bio.

Adding A Personal Note To Your Bio: Useful Or Useless?

Sharing a little bit of personal information in your author bio creates a clearer picture of who you are as a person and a writer. But how much is too much? When is it appropriate to include some personal information, and when does it just make a writer look silly?

Including Personal Information: A Best-Case Scenario
In theory, the perfect author bio contains a brief overview of the author's education (formal or informal), good publishing credits that are listed in the best order, and a sentence that adds a personal touch to an otherwise flat bio.

Adding a personal element to your bio can be informative and helpful to a literary agent—especially if your personal element relates to the book you're pitching. These days, writers are expected to be able to sustain a social media following. And the more interesting you are as a person, the more likely you'll be able to attract fans online.

When possible, try to tie your personal element into your writing life. Here are some examples:

Talk about the people you live with.
Example: *I live with my husband and three children under the age of six—and I never lack inspiring stories, thanks to them!*

Talk about your hobbies.
Example: *When I'm not writing, I enjoy fly-fishing, pottery, and hiking to help me stay inspired.*

Talk about places where you have lived or traveled.
Example: *I have lived in Japan, Nepal, and Spain, and my travels continue to inspire my writing.*

Talk about your out-of-work interests.
Example: *When I'm not writing, I like to volunteer at my local library by reading stories during children's hour.*

But Wait—Don't Some People Say That Adding A Personal Line To A Bio Is Not Very Helpful?
There are agents who don't care if you live with your dog or enjoy planting flowers. However, we've learned that these people are the exceptions. Most agents enjoy learning a little bit about you.

Is a line about your personal life necessary in your bio? Not always. Does it hurt to include a personal element? We don't think so. We believe a personal touch in your query letter can only help.

The Right Way To Use Your Pen Name In Your Cover Or Query Letter

Should you include your real name in a query or cover letter?

Yes. Absolutely. Here's the rule of thumb:

- *Submit* work and do business under your real name.
- *Publish* under your pen name.

All dealings with agents, editors, publicists, and other industry professionals should be conducted under your real name. Why? Because it's good business. Think about it this way: "Pen name" is a nice way of saying "fake name." And there are very few of us who use aliases in our everyday lives.

You wouldn't introduce yourself at a job interview using a fake name, and since a query letter acts as an introduction, the same rules apply. Using your real name suggests that you're honest and open—not trying to hide anything. Honesty is always the best policy.

Plus, if your literary agent is going to draw up a contract or write a check for you, he or she would use your real name.

Where in a query letter should you mention a pen name?
One sentence at the end of the bio section of your query letter mentioning that you write under a specific pen name should be sufficient. *Only* include your pen name if you've already been published under that pen name. If you do not have any writing credentials with a pen name, it's best to leave it out and wait to discuss with a lit agent upon further interest in your writing.

Where on a manuscript should you write a pen name?
In your submissions to agents, you'll want to include your *real* name with your contact information on the first page (typically upper left corner) of your manuscript.

Then, when you write the title, you can do something like:

The Best Story Ever Written
by
Arabella Von Pseudonym

There are no hard-and-fast rules about pen name format on manuscripts: The important thing is to be sure to distinguish your real name from your pen name—and to always associate with fellow professionals using your real name, but to publish under your pen name.

Element #5: Knowing How To Say Goodbye

Congratulations!

You've completed four important elements of your query letter (salutation, intro, blurb, and bio). And now let's look at the fifth element: your closing lines.

It's important to express your gratitude in a sincere way. Thank the agent for his or her time and consideration. Do not make demands on turnaround time (*I'll expect an answer in two weeks*) or come across as pushy (*I'll call next Friday to see what you think*).

If you are submitting in hard copy, you might want to make a note that you have included an SASE (self-addressed stamped envelope), but it isn't really necessary (most will assume and/or see that you've included it). Editors and agents will know whether or not you want your work returned by the size of the envelope and the amount of postage.

Then, close your letter with "sincerely" or "regards" or any other word that best represents you. The good people at About.com offer this handy list of letter closings:

- Regards
- Best
- Best regards
- Kind regards
- Yours truly
- Most sincerely
- Respectfully
- Respectfully yours
- Sincerely
- Thank you
- Thank you for your consideration

TMI: 10 Things NOT To Say In Your Query Letter

Once your "sincerely" has been placed at the bottom of your letter, there are a few things you'll want to edit for. One of them is TMI (too much information).

We writers can either be closed off and private, or very prone to over-sharing. When you submit your writing, you want to be sure you're not sharing TMI. Here are a few things you should consider leaving out of your query letters.

1. **Age at which you started writing.** If you're making submissions, it's pretty much a given that at some point in your life, you began to love writing. Maybe you were five and maybe you were fifty. Unless there's an especially compelling and relevant reason to mention when or why you fell for writing, best to leave it out.

2. **Number of places the work has already been rejected.** If you were walking into a restaurant and everyone who was leaving stopped to tell you how uninteresting and bland the food was, would you sit down at a table and ask for a menu? Probably not.

3. **The reason you don't think the work will be picked up.** There's no point in mentioning that your writing may be weak. If it is weak, the work will speak for itself.

4. **How much money you expect/want to make.** A query or cover letter is not the place to talk about payment, advances, or rights (like movie deals). Have that discussion once you're further along in the process.

5. **When you had your last eye exam.** Unless your medical condition is relevant to your writing, it may not be appropriate to mention any mental or physical health issues in your letter.

6. **How many of your friends and family members like your writing.** Praise from blood relations, in-laws, friends, and writing groups doesn't count when you're gunning for the big leagues. Include only professional reviews or quotes from established writers.

7. **Personal manifestos.** You certainly can (and should) have a personal manifesto (or two). But your letter is not the place to mention it unless it ties directly into your writing.

8. **Negative situations with other publishing professionals.** Don't complain about past editors or agents in your query; it could make you look like a writer who is difficult to work with.

9. **This is my [first/second/thirtieth] manuscript.** While feeling proud of your accomplishments is good, literary agents or editors will likely read that you've written thirty books and wonder why none of them have been published. And if it's your first or second manuscript, that may not be something to call attention to either.

10. **This is the first of a completed, fifteen-book series.** If you've written fifteen books in a series but you haven't sold the first one yet, you may be in for trouble if you mention it in your query. We'll say more about this in Part Six: Custom Designs For Special Query Letters.

The Moral Of The Story For Your Letters

Writing a query letter is like going on a job interview: you don't want to give too much or too little information. Always speak to your strengths, not your weaknesses. Common sense and a bit of smart self-editing will go a long way!

Your Query Letter Checklist

- Is the query letter professional-looking? Carefully proofread, free of typos, and in an easy-to-read font like Times New Roman?
- Have you included current and correct contact information?
- Have you defined your genre?
- Is the letter one page of clear, concise writing?
- Have you demonstrated enthusiasm for your work?
- Have you addressed your letter to the right person and double-checked the spelling of his or her name?
- Have you thanked the agent for his or her time?
- Have you kept a log of your submissions to prevent confusion later?

Part Four

How To Assemble An Attention-Getting Summary For Your Nonfiction Book

How To Assemble An Attention-Getting Summary For Your Nonfiction Book

The Best Way To Structure Your Self-Help And How-To Summary

In the world of popular nonfiction (as opposed to academic or scholarly nonfiction), self-help or how-to books are meant to change readers' lives for the better. But that's not an easy promise to make!

Here's the best book blurb structure to use when writing your persuasive pitch:

1. Lay out the primary problem. Open with the main problem your book addresses. If you can make a strong case explaining why your book is the best solution to that problem—and that lots of people will clamor to buy it—the more likely it is that an agent will pay attention.

Note: We're making up our own statistics here just to prove a point.

Example of laying out the primary problem: *Every year, 500,000 Americans buy one million dollars' worth of books on diets that they probably don't follow. With conflicting reports about what's good to eat and what's not, readers are looking for a simple diet plan that offers fast, easy results.*

2. Show how your book proposes the best, most ingenious solution to the problem. Don't make vague statements. Your specific problem requires a specific solution.

Example: *My book, THE LIMA BEAN DIET, is the first book to take this simple vegetable and use it in an easy-to-follow diet plan that gets results with no hunger and NO complicated calorie- or carb-counting.*

3. Present your talking points and headlines. What specific elements of your book could capture media attention? The more practical and applicable your advice, and the more surprising your solution, the more you'll stand out.

Example: *The lima bean is a hugely misunderstood food, mocked by comedians and scorned by foodies. Few people realize that it's actually a superfood packed with appetite-quenching nutrients—and that it takes more energy to digest a lima bean than is contained in the bean itself! So eating lima beans actually makes a person lose weight.**

*Note: As far as we know, this is totally untrue. But you get the point. Your angle has to be new and surprising. Take our advice about query letters, not diets!

4. Explain how your book is different from every other book available on your topic. If you're writing in a competitive field (like health or spirituality), then you should mention why *your* book is unique within the marketplace. Focus on what's lacking in existing books on your subject. Be specific! But remember: You can go into more detail in your formal proposal.

Example: *Books like THE POTATO DIET have made similar claims, but didn't catch on because they lacked the simplicity and nutritional magic of my breakthrough diet plan.*

5. Say why you're the right person to write your book. In self-help and how-to, who you are as a writer can't be separated from what you're writing about. Why are *you* the most qualified writer for this unique book? Your author bio should demonstrate a willingness and ability to support your message with a strong author platform.

Example: *As a world-famous doctor of Beanology, I'm the top expert on lima beans. Let me tell you about my awesome bean research awards...*

6. Include information about who your target readers are. Consider offering comparison titles or specific details about the audience that would be interested in your book.

Example: *Readers of THE POTATO DIET, and diet books in general, will be interested in this revolutionary, never-before-seen concept in dieting.*

Here's what the book blurb would look like in full:
Every year, 500,000 Americans buy one million dollars' worth of books on diets that they probably don't follow. With conflicting reports about what's good to eat and what's not, readers are looking for a simple diet plan that offers fast, easy results. My book, THE LIMA BEAN DIET, is the first book to take this simple vegetable and use it in an easy-to-follow diet plan that gets results with no hunger and NO complicated calorie- or carb-counting.

The lima bean is a hugely misunderstood food, mocked by comedians and scorned by foodies. Few people realize that it's actually a superfood packed with appetite-quenching nutrients—and that it takes more energy to digest a lima bean than is contained in the bean itself! So eating lima beans actually makes a person lose weight.

Books like THE POTATO DIET have made similar claims, but didn't catch on because they lacked the simplicity and nutritional magic of my breakthrough diet plan. *As a world-famous doctor of Beanology, I'm the top expert on lima beans. Let me tell you about my awesome bean research awards…*

What Not To Say
Don't point out the obvious. We've read many query letters in which writers point out the popularity of things that are *obviously* popular. Unless you can offer some surprising, eye-catching information that directly ties into your book, don't waste agents' time telling them what they already know. Use surprising facts only to make a point about why your book is going to sell.

Weak:
>Every year, thousands of people die in car crashes.

Stronger:
>Every year, X number of people die or are injured from car crashes related to texting.

Weak:
>The health food industry is one of the biggest in the nation, so people will read my new book, *The Lima Bean Diet*.

Stronger:
>Surveys from Big-Name University suggest consumers have an increased skepticism about the claims of low-carb diets; my new Lima Bean Diet speaks to former and current low-carbers, as well as all natural-food lovers.

Weak:
>People love cop shows on TV. Newspapers report lots of crime stories. Therefore, readers will want to hear about my solutions to the crime epidemic.

Stronger:
>As you know, interest in true crime stories continues to surge, and readers will be intrigued by my radical approach to ending crime, which is detailed through my true stories of criminal rehabilitation.

How To Write A Successful Summary For Biography, History, And Popular Science

If you've written a biography, history book, or popular science book, your query letter will face challenges that a query for a novel or memoir will not. The two most important factors in your query are your book blurb (the description of your book) and your author bio. For pop science, history, biography, and books of that nature, your query must present the credentials that establish you as an expert (or forthcoming expert) in your field, and it should wow agents with the promise of a "never been done this way before" premise.

Your Book Premise: Key Elements To Summarizing And Selling Your Book Idea

Usually, books in the genres we're discussing are submitted to publishers as a book proposal. Occasionally, a writer will complete the manuscript first, but most of the time, what you're actually pitching is a formal and extensive proposal for a book, as opposed to the finished, complete book.

Here are the key points to highlight when writing the 150- to 200-word book summary in your query:

Introduce your book idea with a dazzling new perspective.
Consider your angle: What makes your book different? Appealing? Tease those elements out in your introductory line.

> Example: Think you know everything about Thomas Jefferson? Think again! My book, *THE PIRATE PARADE*, researched over my many years as a scholar at School Name Here, proves that our third president not only engaged with pirates on the Barbary Coast; he became one!

The staying power (or trendiness) of your subject.
There are oodles of biographies on Thomas Jefferson—and that's great! Any halfway savvy agent will be familiar with the subject without you needing to reveal there's an audience for your book. But if your subject is a little more off the beaten path, you might need to make a careful case for its popularity. Don't overdo it! The more it seems like you're struggling to prove that your book will be popular, the less likely it is that you'll find an excited audience.

> Example: Tea gets a rap for being as egregiously uncool as teapot cozies knit by Grandma. But the true story of tea is one of war, sex,

spies, illicit affairs, conspiracy, and intrigue. My book, *The Tea Revolution*, is the steamy tell-all that the one billion tea drinkers of America have been waiting for.

What's different about your book?
If you've written yet another biography of Thomas Jefferson to add your ideas to the many portrayals already out there, you've got to explain why your book is different from what people have already read. We're illustrating this in the examples above. Who knew Thomas Jefferson was a pirate?* Who knew tea could be so sexy?**

*He wasn't a pirate.
**Is tea sexy? Depends on who you ask.

What are your talking points?
Tease out the elements that are the most media-friendly. Here are some elements of your book to consider highlighting in your query:

- *Surprise!* Elements: Something readers haven't seen or considered before.

- Human Elements: Topics that will rouse the emotions or speak to universal truths.

- Trendy or Timely Elements: What readers want/need to know because they have immediate bearing on current hot-button topics.

- Contradictory Elements: Information that goes against commonly held beliefs.

- Warning/Whistle-Blower Elements: Details that are so essential to know, people will *have* to buy the book.

Your Nonfiction Author Bio
For any nonfiction subjects, you must have a strong bio. Agents (and publishers, and readers) won't take your research and writing seriously if you can't demonstrate that you are a trusted source of information. Without an established background that proves your expertise, it's unlikely you'll find a publisher.

To develop the kind of track record that's going to allow an agent or publisher to put faith in you as an expert, follow this checklist. You don't have to cover ALL of the points noted, but the more you can check off, the better your odds of getting a traditional book deal for your nonfiction project. Here are the elements agents look for in a nonfiction query letter.

- Authorship of feature articles on your subject or related subjects. The more well-known the publication, the better.

- Having a blog—specifically if it's popular.

- Your articles appear on other people's blogs and online newspapers. While you might not get paid, you'll definitely build your reputation.

- Education, a degree, and—if applicable—that you give lectures and present papers on your subject.

- Publication in the literary journal market. Lit mags often feature narrative nonfiction essays on various subjects that have wide appeal.

- Media experience. Radio and TV appearances will give you some street cred.

3 Examples Of Awesome Bios For Nonfiction Writers

Example #1: For a book about the history of cooking

I've been working in the food services industry for twenty years, and I've been writing as a food critic for Major Magazine Name *for the past three years. My popular blog has been featured in XYZ magazine, and I've been teaching cooking classes at Fancy Cooking School for ten years. I've been a regular speaker at the Farm to Food Conference for three years running, with standing-room-only audiences. To get to know me, please check out my Facebook page: www.adddress.com or my author website: www.address.com.*

Example #2: For a book about meditation for teenagers

I first became interested in meditation when I myself was a teenager and needed to find a peaceful place in a not-so-peaceful home. Since then, I've become a certified meditation teacher with Famous School, where I had the pleasure of studying with Name of Famous Guru (note: Name of Famous Guru may be willing to write the introduction for my book, if it is accepted for publication). Now I run a busy website that helps parents teach meditation strategies to at-risk teens, and I am the founder of the Teen Meds Center in Town, State, where I work regularly with struggling teens and where I also host retreats and seminars for educators who want to build meditation into their curriculum. My writings on teenagers and meditation have appeared in Major Parenting Magazine Names Here.

Example #3: For a book about having a happy marriage

Initially, most of my interest in learning how to cultivate a happier marriage stemmed from the difficulties my own parents—and later, my husband and I—had. My instincts were good, but I cultivated them by taking classes at Name of School to become a certified social worker with an emphasis on marriage counseling. Now I travel regionally presenting my sold-out seminars at hotels and libraries. I've appeared as an expert on NPR and my local news station. When the self-published edition of my book hit the Amazon best-seller lists, I thought it might be time to explore the possibility of traditional publication to share my advice and tips with a greater audience. To learn more, please visit my website: www.address.com.

Strategies For Pitching Your Nonfiction Book: It's A Personal Thing

Any query letter for popular nonfiction can offer a handful of facts about your proposed book—and most stop there. But your query letter will be more likely to stand out if you give it a personal touch.

Make It Personal

Self-help and how-to book authors are expected to become celebrities in their fields, especially on social media. This means that your story—your personal story about who you are and what your experiences have been—matters. It's part of your author platform.

Consider the various *American Idol* and *Dancing With The Stars* genres of television shows. Producers could have simply featured dancers and singers in side-by-side comparisons with no backstory. Instead, they show not only the singing or dancing, but also small vignettes about each performer's family life, hopes, fears, and struggles. It's the personal element—the likability factor—that gives a competitive edge.

The same theory applies to popular nonfiction books (and also, to some extent, novels and memoirs). If you have a compelling personal backstory, show it off in your query letter. Why are you writing this particular book? What adversity have you overcome?

Make An Emotional Appeal To Your Audience

The reason that a personal backstory can be so engaging is that true stories of hope and inspiration capture our emotions. They tug our heartstrings; they make us laugh, cry, and share the hopes of the storyteller.

Your book pitch can do the same thing for literary agents. What can you include in your book summary to encourage a strong emotional response to your book premise? Can you make them feel a spark of hope for the solution to their problems? Or does your book make them sympathize with you?

Examples Of Emotional And Unemotional Book Blurbs

Example 1: Just the facts.
My book, THE LIMA BEAN DIET, offers readers an alternative to traditional diet books, which tend to be convoluted, complex, overly detailed, and confusing. Readers will enjoy learning how to lose weight an easier way.

How To Assemble An Attention-Getting Summary For Your Nonfiction Book

Example 2: Make it personal.
I'm a food scientist by trade, having spent fifteen years working for a major ice-cream manufacturer. And in the last decade, I gained 100 pounds. Like so many others who are overweight, I felt frustrated, tired, and confused by the excessive number of convoluted diet fads out there.

That's why I created The Lima Bean Diet. It's an easy, wholesome diet based on my years of scientific, professional research—and it gets results. As a person who knows what it's like to eat nothing but ice cream all day long, I believe the Lima Bean Diet is the answer that dieters have been waiting for.

Example 3: More facts.
My book, HOW TO THINK LIKE YOUR DOG, offers the reader a glimpse into the mind of his or her dog. Often, the problem with most human-canine relationships is a language barrier; humans don't speak dog. The result is a dysfunctional relationship that doesn't make anybody happy.

My book teaches readers to interpret their dogs' body language to better understand what they're thinking. The result? Better human-dog relationships.

Example 4: Make it personal.
A professional dog-trainer of forty years with countless publications under my belt, I've seen just about every kind of human-canine "language barrier" issue out there. So when my friend Lew told me he was having problems with his couch-chewing, leash-pulling spaniel, I decided to give him an early copy of my manuscript HOW TO THINK LIKE YOUR DOG. The result? Lew's pup no longer chews the couch, messes on the floor, or barks excessively. He's not my first client to get results from my groundbreaking method, but he's the first to get results simply from reading my book!

Will an emotional/personal appeal ALWAYS work? Is it always necessary?

Every book is unique. Some books, especially those of a more academic or scholarly bent, might not lend themselves to a strong emotional appeal. And trying to force an emotional or personal element when there simply isn't one could (and probably would) backfire.

Trust your instincts to present the best possible description of your nonfiction book in your query letter. And no matter what your angle, let your enthusiasm for your subject always lead the way!

A Sample Query Letter For Nonfiction That Worked

To us, a successful query is one that causes a literary agent to request more materials: sample pages, a synopsis, or the complete manuscript. The query letter included in this section was successfully used by a Writer's Relief client who allowed us to publish it here for your review.

We hope you'll enjoy!

Dear Agent:

I hope you'll consider representing my new self-help book, *The Message In Migraine*.

I am a writer with an extensive publishing background, particularly in the health and natural healing fields (Rodale, Inc.), as well as nature and science (Time-Life). My nonfiction credits include a history book (Donning Press) and a social studies text on the country of Burundi (Chelsea House). My articles have appeared in *Prevention, Vegetarian Times, Healthy Woman, Heart & Soul, Healthy You, Berks County Living Magazine,* and other magazines.

Migraines afflict an estimated 37 million Americans, most of them women, and I was one of them. So many of us have turned to modern medicine for relief, only to be disappointed by ineffective pills and expensive treatments that don't work. My book offers migraine sufferers what they really need: a way to interpret the messages of migraines and access the physician within.

The Message In Migraine differs from current and previous migraine titles by directly addressing the deepest underlying origin of the body's pain: a misalignment of body, mind, and spirit. Drawing on cutting-edge research in alternative therapies, I offer readers a practical roadmap that teaches sufferers how to "read" the messages in their headaches. Then I offer a customizable plan to help them create their own unique wellness program that treats body, mind, and spirit in symphony to relieve pain.

Thank you kindly for your consideration. Please do not hesitate to request a sample chapter.

Sincerely,

Marian Frances Wolbers
www.marianwolbers.com

Part Five

Support Materials

Sample Pages, Synopses,
And Formal Book Proposals

Support Materials For Fiction And Memoir

When querying an agent or editor with a completed novel or memoir, only include sample pages *if the submission guidelines state that additional materials are welcome.*

Otherwise, have your support materials ready for immediate review the moment you begin sending out your query letters. If an agent requests additional materials, you'll need to send them (usually by email) right away. Delaying overly long could cast a negative light on your prospects, since agents expect to work with writers who are punctual and prepared.

Your Synopsis: Writing It Doesn't Have To Be A Chore

Writers of novels and memoirs often hate the job of writing a book synopsis. They agonize over every sentence: *What is a literary agent looking for in my synopsis or summary? How many details should I include? Should I explain my setting and characters or just stick to the basic plot?*

Let's start with the fundamentals.

What Is A Synopsis For A Book Or Novel?

A synopsis is different than a book blurb. A book blurb is a short, teasing summary of your story included in the query letter. A synopsis is a longer, one- to two-page, detailed description of the entire story. A synopsis may accompany your query letter or be sent later if the agent requests additional information about your book. Generally speaking, a full-length synopsis is usually requested from writers who are working in the genre of fiction or memoir.

1. How should you format the pages of your synopsis? Write your synopsis in the same format as your manuscript. If you aren't familiar with industry-standard formatting, contact us via our website (WritersRelief.com) for free guidelines.

2. How should you begin your synopsis? Begin by broadly describing your story in twenty-five words or less, if possible. You must capture the agent's attention.

3. What verb tense should you use for your synopsis? Write in present tense. Focus on major plot points or turning points. Omit secondary characters, subplots, and minor events. Don't go into too much detail.

4. What should you focus on in your synopsis? Include the setting, main characters, and the all-important CONFLICT. Then, show the resolution of this conflict.

5. Should you tell the ending of your book in your synopsis? Yes. Include a COMPLETE summary of your story from beginning to end. We know you want to keep readers guessing, but the novel synopsis is not the place for it. Leave the teasing for the book blurb in your query letter!

6. Should you ask rhetorical questions in your synopsis to keep readers interested? No. Do not ask empty questions in your synopsis. Doing so will not fool the agent into asking for the remaining pages of your manuscript.

7. Does proofreading really matter in your synopsis? Absolutely! Proofread your synopsis. Make sure grammar, punctuation, and spelling are perfect.

8. Should you write your synopsis in first person from a character's perspective or third person? Write your synopsis in third person for a novel. If you are writing a memoir, use the same tense as what you use in your book.

9. How long is a synopsis for a novel? There are no industry-wide rules at this point to dictate the length of your synopsis. Each agent will have a different preference. Our advice: Limit your synopsis to one or two pages (three at most). In our experience, it's better to come in under the requested page count than over.

The 5 Most Common Synopsis Mistakes

There's a little repetition in this list, but we wanted you to clearly see the most common synopsis mistakes:

5. Choosing the wrong verb tense. A synopsis should be written in present tense. There are almost no exceptions to this rule.

4. Not showing a clear plot arc. Sometimes writers will mention what seems like an important plot point (hero resents father who misses the big game; child can't find her beloved dog), but then the issue never appears to resolve. If you pick up the thread of one plot element or subplot, your synopsis should show that your book offers a conclusion. Also, be sure that the pacing of your main conflict has lots of forward momentum and shape, especially if you're writing in a traditional genre.

3. Not offering clear transitions. Yes, we know that A in your story is followed by B. But...why? For example: A dying woman leaves her estate to the wrong son. The other son, who believes he should have inherited everything, leaves the country. What's missing here? You got it: the cause part of "cause and effect." Why did she leave everything to the first son? Unless you're writing a mystery (in which case it helps to deliberately draw attention to unsolved questions), always explain.

2. Lazy writing. All the important rules about writing fiction—using the five senses for evocative prose, showing instead of telling, establishing character, etc.—apply to synopsis writing. Convinced that their book's manuscript pages will be good enough to entice a literary agent, many writers just haphazardly throw together a quickly written synopsis. A synopsis should be carefully written to engage, compel, and bring the story to life.

And the number one, most common mistake writers make when writing a synopsis for a novel...

1. Not giving away the ending. There may be no greater mark of the amateur novelist than a writer who turns in a synopsis to a literary agent with a "cliffhanger ending." The point of a synopsis is to tell the full story so an agent knows what he or she is agreeing to represent. Your synopsis should always provide the full scope of your story, beginning to end.

Other Common Synopsis Mistakes For Book Writers:

- Switching POV (from first to third person)
- Bad, overcomplicated formatting
- Focusing on too many subplots
- Introducing too many minor characters and their names
- Going on too long

Writing a synopsis for a book is hard; mistakes happen. You may need to rewrite your synopsis multiple times before you're satisfied with the results. Ask yourself: If a literary agent had ONLY your synopsis to go on in order to make a decision about your book, would he or she love it? If the answer is "yes," then your synopsis is ready.

Prepare Your Book's Opening Pages

If a literary agent requests your opening pages along with your query (some do!), then you'll need to ensure that your writing sample is engaging. Your query and supporting materials will often need to work hand in hand.

When an agent requests sample pages, he or she always means the *first* pages of your book. Don't send pages from the middle unless specifically requested to do so.

Excuses, Excuses

Although most writers know that their opening pages need to be stellar, some writers have trouble *accepting* that, and doing something about it.

Some writers push themselves to write a compelling opening—even to the point of rewriting the entire book. But other writers tend to go easier on themselves. "If only the literary agent would read the second chapter," they say. "That's when the book gets interesting."

The fact is, few (if any) literary agents will read beyond a slow opening in the hopes that the book gets better. If you find yourself making excuses for your opening pages, it may be time to face the truth: The better your opening, the better your shot at getting an agent.

Two Common Opening Styles To Avoid

There are a number of opening gambits that writers would be wise to avoid. Here are two we see frequently:

Unnecessary prologues. Most prologues do little to grab a reader's attention—they're big and splashy but often lack substance and are inappropriate for the tone of the book. Sometimes they can be effective hooks, but if you're determined to use a prologue, make sure it's necessary and consistent with the tone of the rest of your book.

Backstory. Some book openings are bogged down by long passages that recall everything that happened before the present action of the story actually begins. As a result, the plotline doesn't get interesting until a dozen (or more) pages into the book. However, the reader often quits reading long before reaching that point. Writers sometimes find it difficult to understand where their narrative should begin. They spend a lot of time describing things that happened in the past. But the power of a story lies in how it looks forward, not back.

For example: A writer is composing a story about a cop whose unusual approach to solving crime stems from his experiences a few years ago when his own home was burglarized. A new writer—thinking linearly—might be inclined to begin the narrative at the beginning, starting with the cop's house being robbed and showing his evolution toward his particular kind of crime fighting. But a veteran writer would start in the present—a cop fighting crime in an unusual way—and then weave in the backstory as needed.

Here Are Four Tips To Keep In Mind For The First Five Pages Of Your Novel Or Memoir:

1. Opening Action

Your opening pages must grab or hook the reader. One of the best ways to do this is to start with an intense and important moment. It doesn't have to be a momentous save-the-world crisis; it could be something as small as a fifth grader trying to figure out where to sit in the cafeteria.

What's essential is that you invest the moment with gravity and consequence. The character might be on the brink of real change or perhaps facing a decision that will affect the people in his or her life. Whatever you open with, make it clear that it's important—vitally important—to the entire plot to come.

2. Characters

Of course, whichever character you choose to focus on should be fascinating. Show the reader right away why it's worth spending time with your character. Is she courageous and selfless? Excellent! Readers want to spend time with heroes and heroines they admire. Is he devious, sinister, and complex? Perfect! We love villains who are multidimensional, who believe they're doing right—or who can't stop themselves from doing wrong.

Your characters must draw your audience in. Show the reader what your characters want, and present a scene in which they are trying to get it.

NOTE: Be careful that you don't introduce too many characters at once. Hook your reader with ONE character first, and don't introduce any other characters until you've set the hook in deep.

3. Setting

Choosing a unique, larger-than-life, out-of-the-ordinary setting for your opening pages will offer a higher interest factor. Rendering your setting in distinct detail will draw the reader into your world. Open your book somewhere your readers have never been, and lure them in.

BUT—if your opening isn't set in Antarctica or the forgotten storeroom of a traveling Believe-It-Or-Not show, don't fret. What's important is to present your setting in a way that will make something about it surprising or new to your readers. You may have an opening scene in a familiar landscape—say, the cafeteria again—but it's how you render the scene that can make it amazing and fascinating. Use the POV (point of view) of your character to offer details that the reader may have taken for granted, details that are quietly amazing.

4. Momentum

Perhaps what's most crucial about your first scene is its momentum—the force that propels readers into the next page, and the next, and the next. Your opening pages should NOT be *answering* questions about your character's quest or your character's past. The opening should be *asking* them.

Think of your opening pages as the open door to your book. Your task is to invite and intrigue the reader and get them to come inside—and you can't do that without creating a sense of anticipation. So don't offer all your resolutions in the first pages. Tempt the reader to read on.

Support Materials For Nonfiction Book Proposals: Self-Help, How-To, Biography, Popular Science, etc.

If you're pitching nonfiction that isn't memoir, then you already know you don't necessarily have to finish your book before an agent can help you get a publisher for it.

But you DO need to complete your formal book proposal. This can be an intense and time-consuming effort. Some writers spend as much time on their proposals as on their books.

Your nonfiction book proposal is a persuasive and comprehensive summary of the specs of your project. We could write an entire book on how to craft a good nonfiction book proposal.

For our purposes in this book, we'll touch on the fundamental elements of a formal book proposal that you'll need to have ready before your query letter is sent.

Nonfiction Book Proposal Components:

Title Page:
In your nonfiction proposal, start with your name and contact information, an approximate word count, and the proposed title of your work. Make sure your main title describes the subject matter of the book and, if possible, don't rely on subtitles to convey vital information—subtitles are often dropped in computerized listings and library databases. Note: The title you choose is your "working title," as publishers may elect to change it.

Summary (also known as the overview, synopsis, or executive summary) —one page maximum:
Begin with a very short description of your book's basic premise. Whatever makes your book stand out should be highlighted in the first few sentences.

Capture the agent's attention and make it clear what you're selling. If the agent has to hunt around for the point of your book, he or she is likely to toss the proposal aside and review the next proposal in the towering pile.

Chapter-by-Chapter Outline—one to two paragraphs per chapter:
Create a dynamic outline by highlighting each chapter's major points. Each chapter synopsis should be no longer than one or two paragraphs; you don't want to give too much information, but you don't want to give too little either.

Emphasize each chapter's unique and/or important function in relation to the rest of the book. By the time the agent has read this outline, he or she should have a clear idea of the overall book.

The Market For Your Nonfiction Book:
This section should include information about the book's intended audience and how your book uniquely addresses the needs of that particular audience. Make sure your market is clear (as in "women ages 30–60," or "the 200,000 people who buy antique cars each year") and provide as many demographics as possible about your targeted audience. Include observations about current trends that favor your book, and highlight what makes your book marketable.

Competing Titles:
Include information about the competition. If other books on the same subject exist, yours must offer a new or original take. Identify and describe any current books that are similar, then explain how yours fills a specific niche.

Author Information:
List your education, writing credentials, contacts, experience—whatever makes you uniquely qualified to write your book. You should also offer details about your existing author platform: where you've been asked to speak as an expert on your subject, how many fans/friends you have on social media, etc.

Marketing And Publicity Plan:
You will also need to outline your own future promotional ideas and resources to help market the book. Include details about affiliations, contacts, or endorsements you may have lined up. Do you have a prominent person willing to write the foreword? Media contacts? A website or newsletter? Possible sequels or spin-off information should be included in this section.

Specifications Of Your Unfinished Book:
Outline an approximate word count, the number of chapters, and an estimated completion time frame. Mention if your book will contain any charts, photographs, or illustrations. You may also describe the general format you envision. However, be prepared to be flexible when it comes to length and format—the publisher will have the final say. The word count for nonfiction can vary greatly by subject and intention, but on average, a full-length book is approximately 80,000-100,000 words.

Sample Chapters:
If you have already begun the writing process, send one or two completed chapters (chapters one and two are preferable, but not mandatory).

Other Tips:

- Your book proposal should be similar in style to your proposed book. If your book is meant to be humorous and lighthearted, make sure your proposal is written in the same style.
- Make sure the proposal is thoroughly edited and proofread. Literary agents admit to passing over potentially great ideas if they find errors, typos, and coffee stains.
- Always include an SASE for responses. Or know the etiquette for submitting online.
- Use industry-standard formatting. Contact us at WritersRelief.com for guidelines, if you need them.

Part Six

Custom Designs For Special Query Letters

Querying With Fictionalized Nonfiction (or Nonfiction-y Fiction)

Sometimes it's hard to know whether to market a book as fiction or nonfiction. Here are some fiction-y nonfiction (or nonfiction-y fiction) scenarios we've run into, along with suggestions for identifying the genre in query letters.

SCENARIO ONE. The author has written a book based on his life. The story is faithful to his experiences in the way that all creative nonfiction tries to recreate stories from memories as accurately as possible. The author has changed the characters' names to protect identities, but otherwise everything is true. (Writer's Relief tip: Changing a person's name will not necessarily protect you from a lawsuit if your characters are inspired by real people.)

The problem: The author values his life experience and wants to pitch his book as a memoir. But the names have been changed, so in that way, it's not entirely truthful.

Solution: In your query letter, include: *My book is an accurate memoir of my life story, though I have changed some names.*

SCENARIO TWO. An author has written a book based loosely on her life. The story is very familiar to her because she has lived much of it. She has changed characters' names. She has also taken liberties here and there in order to make the story more compelling, and she amped up the ending to be a little flashier.

The problem: The writer knows that small parts of her tale are fictionalized (perhaps she added a pet dog, a villain, or a love interest), but the larger story is mostly true. Because her real-life experience is so out of the ordinary, she feels it's important that readers understand that the things she's writing about actually happened to her (for the most part). Is this a memoir or a novel? Fiction or nonfiction?

Solution: In this case, we feel the author would be best served by calling her story a novel. Memoir promises truth, and so if the book is not as truthful as the author can possibly make it, then it is not a memoir. In her professional writer's biography, the author might note that her own story is similar to the story of the novel—though not exactly the same.

SCENARIO THREE. A writer has a friend with an unusual life story because she was a professional spy. The writer gets his friend's permission to write a story about everything that happened to her.

The problem: The writer is responsible for what he writes. If the writer's friend is telling him inaccuracies—intentionally or not—the writer will be responsible if/when the book is published. Research is key. All sources must be verified.

Solution: If the writer has done his due diligence and all facts are backed up with proof, then this book might be best pitched as a biography. But if the writer can't attest to the truthfulness of his friend's story, then this book might be best pitched as a novel—and it should probably be quite fictionalized to protect the subjects, the writer, and the publisher.

Still not sure what to call your story?
If you're not sure whether your book is a novel or a memoir, you can always call your project "a story inspired by real-life events" or "a work loosely based on my life." If a literary agent is interested in your project because you've got a strong story and a unique voice, then it's likely he or she will be happy to talk with you about the most appropriate way to publish or pitch it.

THE BOTTOM LINE: Always be honest. If parts of your story are fabricated, say so. If you've changed nothing but names, say that as well. As long as you're being honest, you should be fine.

How And When To Mention Multiple Books (Or A Series) In A Query Letter

Often, writers mention more than one book in a query letter. Sometimes they're letting the agent know that more than one manuscript is available for representation. Other times, they're mentioning additional (past or future) projects in the bio section of the query.

Though every writer's situation is unique, here are some things you'll want to take into account when you mention additional projects in your query letter.

Books designed to be part of a series. Certain books fall into genres that are series-friendly—such as fantasy and mystery novels. If you've written a book in a genre that lends itself well to a series format, then it could be helpful to mention the potential to expand your franchise.

Just be sure that your book *really* is fit for a series: We see far too many books that are not really good candidates for multi-book expansion. Agents often get query letters from writers pitching books as the first in their series that should in fact be stand-alones.

Also, keep in mind that before an agent can sell a second or third book, he or she has to sell the first book. So focus squarely on book one in your query, and then casually mention that the book could be (or is being) developed into a series. If your second, third, and fourth books are already finished and an agent *is* interested in representing you, you can mention your already completed projects once you're in serious discussions.

Vague references to other books. Many writers try to include phrases in their bios such as "I have written five books." This leads the agent to wonder: five published books (why didn't the writer mention the publisher?); five self-published books (what is the writer trying to hide?); or five books that are sitting under a bed somewhere (will the writer try to pawn off those old manuscripts on the agent who takes that writer on?). If the writer is deliberately vague about the "five books," the agent will generally assume the writer is an amateur. Rather than mention you've written five books that you were not able to publish traditionally, it may be better not to mention them at all unless your self-published book has tremendous sales. Focus on building up your bio with publication credits in the literary magazine market or by demonstrating a commitment to your craft.

Spin-offs. Some writers will indicate that they are already in the process of spinning their single-title book into an alternate venture—perhaps developing the story of the secondary characters, or taking the story to the next level with a prequel. Again, be sure you're only pitching one book at a time. If you've already completed your spin-off projects, hold off on mentioning those projects until you and the agent are in serious talks.

Additional projects. Many agents like to know that their potential clients have lots of great ideas for future books. Agents want to invest in long-term partnerships, so they want clients who have lots of ideas. But if you're going to mention additional projects in your query letter, do so carefully. You might consider including a note along the lines of: *Should BOOK TITLE HERE interest you, I would love to speak with you about my ideas for future projects, including my work-in-progress.* But it's best not to dilute the letter's focus on the book you're pitching now.

Other unrelated books or genres. If you're writing a romance novel and you want an agent to work with you on another project (a thriller), the query letter is not the place to mention projects in other genres. If an agent shows interest in one of your projects and you feel you can develop a rapport, you can then mention that you also write in other genres.

THE BOTTOM LINE: A good query letter pitches one book only—in very few special circumstances, it may casually allude to other projects.

Should You Mention Your Self-Publishing History?

If you are submitting a self-published book for consideration so that a literary agent can pitch it to traditional (advance-paying) publishers, you most definitely should mention your self-publishing history *if* you can also mention that the book has been successful in any of the following ways:

- You've sold a substantial number of copies. What constitutes "substantial" varies, but the numbers we've heard indicate about 5,000 sales in one year is worth mentioning. Most self-published books break even, but little more. If you're one of the lucky authors whose self-published book is really selling well, mention your numbers!

- You have received great reviews.

- You have a great quote from another author or publisher.

- You and your book have been featured in various media outlets.

- The book received an award, nomination, or other distinguishing honor.

- It's a regional or niche book which you've marketed to great success.

- Any other interesting acclaim.

When should you NOT mention your book was originally self-published?

Writing a book is a big accomplishment, and self-publishing your work can be an impressive undertaking. However, unless your self-published book has garnered any accolades such as those listed above, it may not be worth mentioning. Here's why:

- Agents want the joy of discovering a new, unpublished book.

- Anyone with a credit card can publish via a self-publishing company, so self-publishing in and of itself is not necessarily a selling point for agents.

- Some writers start their own publishing houses, and that's a huge effort! But taking that approach becomes brag-worthy only if the publishing house turns a profit or garners positive attention. If you've started a successful publishing house, mention your accolades! But remember that it's your *book* that has to appear successful, if that's what you're pitching.

- Mentioning your book was already self-published in your cover or query letter may cause agents to infer that you tried to publish it but ultimately could not find any enthusiasm for your project—even if you didn't attempt the traditional publishing route at all. If you self-published without having first attempted traditional publishing, it's advantageous to mention that.

- If your self-published book has not sold well, an agent may infer that you have not done the necessary legwork to promote your book (and might not do it for future books either); you simply don't know how to promote your book (and might not care to learn); or you did promote your book but didn't get any reader support.

The same recommendations apply to listing any self-published books in your author bio. Be sure your book's title is followed by details about its success.

We want to be clear that we personally support self-published writers; more and more, self-publishing has become a viable avenue to success for some lucky and savvy writers. Agents will consider the merits of self-published novels when sales are strong and there's lots of reader interest.

How To Write A Query For A Self-Published Book

If you've self-published your book and are now seeking a literary agent, you're not alone. In today's volatile publishing industry, many authors are taking the "publish first" approach to getting a book deal. Sometimes this method can lead to a traditional publishing deal. But other times, self-publishing before querying literary agents can make the query process a bit more complicated.

Here are our tips for writing a query letter if you have self-published your book. We often help authors work through the tough decisions needed to make a strong pitch for a self-published book.

SCENARIO ONE: You self-published your book and it took off! You're on the Amazon Best Sellers list. You're getting interview requests. You're making waves.

What your query letter should say: If your book is doing very well, literary agents may come to you! Your query letter should offer specifics about book sales.

SCENARIO TWO: You self-published your book, put a ton of effort into marketing and promoting, and it's doing kind of okay. You have some strong reviews from reputable reviewers (as opposed to random readers or distant cousins). Your author website is getting some interest. Your numbers look promising (you've sold well beyond your friends' friends).

What your query letter should say: Explain why you made the carefully considered choice to self-publish before seeking a traditional publisher, and why you think now is the right time to get a literary agent (maybe signs are pointing toward success, and you want a major publisher to step in).

SCENARIO THREE: You self-published your book with expectations of great wealth and notoriety. You did a little bit of marketing, a few book signings, a little hand-selling, but the story's popularity never grew beyond a few friendly reviews on Amazon. Now you want to ask a literary agent to try to do for the book what you could not: get people to appreciate and buy it.

What your query letter should say: Perhaps this subsection should be called "What your query letter should NOT say." Above all, you want to be positive about your experience. Don't whine. If you're not excited about your book, an agent won't be either. You might want to mention near the end of the letter that you self-published. Or mention it once you're deeper in conversation with an agency.

SCENARIO FOUR: You self-published your book but didn't do any marketing. Perhaps you wanted to get something in print quickly because a loved one was getting on in years. Perhaps you self-published because you wanted to give your book as a gift. Self-publishing was really just a way to share your book with friends and family.

What your query letter should say: If you didn't intend your self-publishing endeavors to reach beyond friends and family, then an agent probably won't hold you accountable for low book sales. Go ahead and mention your "very limited, self-published print run for friends and family."

Sample Query Letter For A Previously Self-Published Book

Here's a query letter we worked on with a Writer's Relief client who had previously self-published. This query successfully spurred agents to request additional materials for the book.

Dear Agent:

I hope you will consider my 53,000-word novel for young children, *The Balloons of Oaxaca*. Set in southeastern Mexico, it is the story of one lonely child's transition into big-city life.

Surviving in a city can seem impossible if you've never seen one before, especially if you're six years old and completely alone. But this is exactly what Utuyu must do when he emerges from The Mountains to the North, where the people do not speak Spanish, and journeys south to the bustling city of Oaxaca, where he can neither speak to the people nor understand them.

Frightened and companionless, Utuyu must be brave and rely on his inner strength to pull him through. Uncommonly resourceful, he solves problems of food and shelter, hygiene and safety, even foiling a wily teenager's attempt to lure him into a life of crime. Will Utuyu find his place in the baffling new city? His adventures make a tale of determination and courage as he learns to cope with feelings all children share.

For many years, I served as vice president for creative projects of Family Communications, Inc., the producers of the landmark children's television series on PBS, *Mister Rogers' Neighborhood*. I received my BA and MA in French and Russian language studies from Oxford University and went on to work as a reporter for *TIME Magazine*. When I left, I established a career as a freelance writer and editor. My fiction and nonfiction have been published in *Harper's*, *Redbook*, *Mademoiselle*, and *Playgirl*. I have coauthored five books through Berkley Books, University of Oklahoma Press, and Winston Press, and was the writer and artistic director of an award-winning television documentary for the *Odyssey* series on PBS. Though I have spent most of my life in the United States, I have retained my British nationality and currently live ten months of the year in Oaxaca, Mexico, where this book takes place. My work has appeared or is forthcoming in *Crack the Spine*.

I self-published *The Balloons of Oaxaca* on a small scale, employing a freelance artist to illustrate the story. It is currently stocked at the preeminent bookstore here in Oaxaca—and the book is always one of their top best sellers.

Custom Designs For Special Query Letters

I hope you might help me introduce the story to a larger audience. The full manuscript is available upon request. Thank you for your time.

Sincerely,

Barry Head

Should You Mention The Freelance Editors, Line Editors, Critique Partners, Ghostwriters, Or Mentors Who Helped You Write Your Book?

It's good to have help on a big project, and writing a book is no exception. But should you mention that someone helped you write your book when you're sending query letters to literary agents? The answer depends on who you are, the type of editing you received, and what you hope your query will accomplish.

Let's look at some of the different avenues writers take when seeking help on a book project, then determine whether it's worth mentioning in a query.

Should you mention in a query that you worked with a content editor?
A content editor is usually a freelance editor who will offer feedback on plot, story, characterization, etc. Content editors offer a broad view of a manuscript, but will sometimes comment on individual passages.

There are two schools of thought on the question of whether to mention freelance editors in a book query. The first is that you should not mention your work with an editor in your query because you don't want the agent to think that the book you're turning in isn't your original book. The agent will have no idea how much of the manuscript is yours and how much stems from the work of a vigorous editor. Also, the agent might wonder why you needed to hire a freelance editor in the first place.

But the second school of thought is that you should mention using a freelance editor because it indicates to agents that you take your craft seriously and are willing to invest in your own writing. It also indicates that an agent may be looking at a better quality submission—a book that has been taken to the next professional level via professional help. Plus, if the literary agent has a relationship with the content editor (many freelancers are ex-editors from publishing houses or ex-agents), then you might have an in.

Generally speaking, you shouldn't mention that you've used a freelance editor in the query letter. Wait until you've already passed the querying stage of a potential relationship. But if you believe your author bio alone isn't strong enough to demonstrate dedication to writing technique and craft, you can let agents know in your query that you worked with a content editor.

Should you mention a line editor in a query letter?
If you've got a great story but aren't so great at composing sentences, then it would make sense to employ a line editor. A line editor cleans up your

grammar, spelling, and sentence structure, but doesn't necessarily offer content editing. An agent would prefer that you hired a line editor if your story is great but your technical skills are lacking.

Is it worth mentioning your line editor in your query, which is the very first thing an agent will use to determine your future relationship? Hiring a line editor isn't something to shout to the rooftops—at least not in a query.

You can (and should) mention your use of a line editor later on, after an agent has been hooked on your book. Once you're having a conversation, and there's an opportunity for an agent to ask questions, then you can mention your line editor and how much he or she did (or didn't) do to your book.

Should you mention a ghostwriter in a query?
A ghostwriter is essentially a non-credited writer who pens the book that will be published under your name.

Most people hire ghostwriters because they themselves are not professional writers—they don't have the instincts or schooling necessary to write in the big leagues. If your author bio is short on credits that suggest you are a professional writer, mentioning your ghostwriter may be a good idea. It will help assure agents that your spectacular story will be told by a spectacular writer.

And if you're putting together a memoir but you yourself are not a writer, agents may be glad to see that you're using a ghostwriter to make the most of your life story. It's fairly common for memoirs and autobiographies to be penned by ghostwriters.

Should you mention a critique partner or mentor who helped with the book?
If your partner or writing mentor is well-known and is amenable to being mentioned in your query, then by all means: drop some names. But if your mentor or critique partner isn't especially well-known, it might not be worth taking up valuable "real estate" in a query that can only be one page long.

How To Write A Query For A Book That Was Previously Represented By An Agent

If you've previously worked with a literary agent (or if you have one now) and you're now looking for a new one using a query letter approach, there are some special considerations you'll want to keep in mind. Every writer's situation is different, and you'll need to consider all aspects of your personal situation when deciding how to write your query letter. But we can offer some tips.

What To Keep In Mind Before You Start Writing Your Query

First things first: check your existing literary agency contract if you have one. Some agent contracts state that you can't look for a new agent while you're still represented by your current one, so you would have to break things off with your current agent before querying others.

You'll have to decide if querying before breaking it off is worth the risk of your current agent finding out that you're looking elsewhere. To reduce the risk of getting a bad reputation in the industry, you might want to query very selectively, as opposed to sending queries to many different agencies all at once.

Also, if an agent has sold a book for you, that agent will most likely be entitled to commissions on the work in perpetuity. Your new agent may not be able to do anything to help you with previously sold books. Starting with a clean slate (and a fresh new book) is generally the best route.

How To Write A Query Letter When You Once Had An Agent But Don't Anymore

Mentioning an "ex" is tricky in any context. Say too much, and you may come across as whiny or bitter. Say too little, and it might seem like you're hiding something.

Unless you have a good, simple reason for having broken things off with your old agency—maybe you quit writing because a family member got sick, or your agency decided to close its doors—then you shouldn't mention your prior agent at all in your query letter. Once a new agent has expressed interest in your manuscript, then it's time to talk in-depth about your publishing history.

If you published books with major publishers in the past, then you don't necessarily need to point out your literary agent history (unless you want to).

The agents who are reading your query letter will recognize that you probably did have literary agent representation at one point. And if/when they want to know more, they'll ask.

How To Write A Query Letter When You Currently Have A Literary Agent But Are Looking For A New One

The best way to begin looking for a new agent is to first sever ties with your old one. But we understand that in the real world, that's not always the route a writer wants to take. Sometimes things just don't work out with a literary agent; maybe the literary agent failed to meet your expectations by sending your book only to a couple of editors—or not sending it out at all. Maybe you feel ignored. You're not totally ready to fire your current agent yet, but you want to put some feelers out about getting a new one.

If your agent HAS NOT yet sent your book out to editors for consideration, you might not need to mention your agency affiliation at all in your query because your book is essentially still new and unseen. HINT: You also might want to fire your current agent ASAP, since the enthusiasm just isn't there. When your agent does start sending your book out, it may make your situation messier and complicate the process of moving from one agency to another. Check out our book *The Writer's Relief Field Guide To Literary Agents* to learn more about how to improve or sever a relationship with a literary agent.

If your current agent has sent your book to a FEW editors, you might choose to be a little vague on your query: "I am currently represented by a reputable literary agency; however, I am seeking a partner who will be able to dedicate more energy and enthusiasm to managing my career. I would be happy to discuss details should my writing interest you."

If your current agent has already sent your book to MANY editors, there may not be much else to do to get your book published. An "imprint" is a publisher's subsidiary that specializes in a certain kind of book. Once an editor at a given imprint has seen your book, it's rare that a different agent will send it to that same imprint again. An agent would be very reluctant to send the same book to a different editor at an imprint if another editor there has already seen it. In other words, getting a new agent to represent a book that a different agent already tried to sell isn't always a viable route unless you've significantly revised the manuscript. Be honest about your book's submission history if you find yourself in talks with a new agent.

Here are some general tips:

Keep it positive. If you had a bad experience with your prior agent, don't lie about it—but don't volunteer anything that could make you look culpable in the failure of the prior relationship.

Don't mention specific agent names. This only makes it easier for your potential agent to contact your old one. If a new agent gets serious about representing you, then you can share your detailed history.

We do NOT recommend putting off discussing your history until after the potential new agent has read your manuscript front to back. If an agent invests time into the book by reading it, but then can't represent it for some reason because of your history, the agent might be irritated with you. And you'll have wasted everyone's time. Mention salient details *after* your query but *before* things go much further.

How To Write A Query For A Short Story Collection

At Writer's Relief, we're approached by countless writers every year who want help submitting their short story collections to literary agents. The short story is an exciting literary form that many writers have mastered, but few writers truly understand how to get a collection of short stories published.

It takes talent and practice to make short stories work. Some novelists begin their careers with stories and work their way up to longer forms (novels or memoirs). Other writers prefer to work in the short form and eventually find themselves with a stack of stories, wondering, "Why not turn my short stories into a collection?"

Short stories are also becoming increasingly popular, because busy people have shorter attention spans. There are hundreds of literary magazines and journals interested in publishing individual stories (and Writer's Relief keeps tabs on all of them), but finding a home for a *collection* of short stories is no easy task.

Major publishers tend to prefer novels. They rarely consider novellas or collections of short stories. Short story collections are also harder to place when the author is not well-known.

Before you protest about the number of successful anthologies on the market, be aware that anthologies are generally collections of stories by a number of different authors and appeal to readers interested in a particular theme or subject matter. Anthologies of work by a single, unknown author are very difficult to sell.

Many writers get frustrated and end up self-publishing their short story collections. But for a writer looking to sell a decent number of books and see his or her collection at the major bookstores, the marketing process can be daunting. When you self-publish, you are responsible for all the marketing and publicity efforts.

Don't let us thoroughly discourage you from trying to get your short story collection traditionally published—there are some things you can do to increase your chances.

Publish selected stories. It's easier to sell a collection if you've had at least a few of the stories previously published in reputable literary journals. Submit individual stories to quality magazines on a regular basis, and with each publication credit, your credibility will increase.

At Writer's Relief we strongly recommend that writers build their credits first rather than approach literary agents with a group of unpublished stories. National exposure in quality magazines is key to attracting an agent's attention.

Theme. It also helps if the stories have a common theme or subject to tie them together. James Herriot was a country vet, not an aspiring author, but his collection of stories had a cohesive theme, and his *All Creatures Great And Small* series is still popular today.

Consider a novel. Some agents recommend scrapping the whole idea of a collection and refashioning it into a novel. They might also recommend selling the collection as part of a two-book deal, with the story collection designed to generate interest in the second book, which would be an actual novel.

Consider a novel-in-stories. If your stories are tightly connected and can be combined to create a larger narrative, you might be able to pitch your collection as a novel-in-stories.

Enter as many short story writing competitions as possible. An award-winning story can land a publishing deal. And it can also boost a writer's self-confidence—always a bonus.

Approach small presses. There are far more small presses than big publishing houses, and they often specialize in niche projects. A small press may be more receptive to a short story collection if they love the quality of your work. You don't necessarily need a literary agent to place your collection with a small press, but you probably will need to send a query letter to the editor, who will then decide whether to request sample pages of your book.

Get schooled. Short story collections are far easier to sell when their authors have top-notch credentials: publication credits in quality magazines, awards, grants. Graduating from a quality MFA program is also a plus.

Sample Query (Short Story Collection)

This Writer's Relief client's short story collection received a lot of positive responses from literary agents; at the time of this writing, it's under consideration at a number of agencies. This client hits all the right notes!

Dear Agent:

Please consider representing my short story collection, *The Power Of Positive Pessimism And Other Stories*.

Now, I realize that the prospect of a short story collection doesn't always make the heart beat faster in eager anticipation. But as my title suggests, negative expectations can often lead to surprisingly positive outcomes.

Why? Of the twenty stories included in this intriguing, eclectic compilation, thirteen have already been accepted and published by well-respected literary journals such as *Bitter Oleander, Westview, Jabberwock Review, RiverSedge, Rougarou,* and *Amarillo Bay,* to name a few. What's more, "And Foolish Notion" was nominated for the Pushcart Prize (2011).

The stories range from comedic, to emotionally affecting, to suspenseful. In "Fortune Cookies," a subway musician makes a deal with the devil, who appears in the form of a Girl Scout. "Compared To What?" tells the story of a washed-up former rock star at the bottom of his career who can still, no matter how horrible the situation, think of something he's been through that was worse. Today's political climate is lampooned in "Out Of Context" when a senator is caught on tape saying something he shouldn't have. And when a noted crossword puzzle constructor suddenly loses the ability to speak or write sentences, it's up to a crossword-loving psychoanalyst to discover why in "Tales From The Cryptic."

The title of the collection comes from my short story of the same name, in which a couple on a blind date discover they have something unique in common: the belief that bad thoughts can lead to good outcomes. Since premonitions rarely come true, why not think of every dreadful possibility you can? It will automatically make it less likely to happen. And that's just what does happen. Sort of.

I attended Brooklyn College and graduated with a BA in speech and theater, then became a recording-studio singer and composer of many successful jingles, including McDonald's, Lipton Tea, and Jeep. I've composed songs and sung backup for Billy Joel, Neil Diamond, Barry Manilow, and Carly Simon, among others. I also performed for a number of years with the improvisational comedy group War Babies.

Complete at 61,839 words, my manuscript is available for your review. Thank you for your time, and I will continue to turn negative thoughts into positives as I await your reply.

Sincerely,

Lenny Levine
www.lennylevinewriter.com

Sample Query (Novel-In-Stories)

This Writer's Relief client received three manuscript requests from agents within twenty-four hours of this query letter being sent out! In this case, the author's short stories came together to form a loose narrative about a single family, so we opted to position the book as a novel-in-stories rather than as a traditional short story collection. For that reason, the book blurb reads more like a novel than a series of stories.

Also, notice the way the author includes her pen name in her bio. If an agent looks for her prior publications, he or she will have to search under the writer's pen name.

Since we felt the collection was a bit on the short side, we suggested putting the word count at the end of the letter, rather than in the first line. The popularity of this pitch shows that even if your word count is a little outside the norm, agents still may be willing to work with you.

Dear Agent,

Please consider representing *The Fire For Lucky Horseshoes*, a novel of interconnected stories about an African-American family who must face the consequences of the patriarch's actions.

Two years after leaving her adulterous husband, Clarisse Knox still can't let go of the past. The town of Sustain, Virginia, is so small, she faces regular run-ins with her ex's mistress and new family—and encounters with Tim himself. Clarisse struggles with her post-divorce life as the mother of two devastated children, a caregiver to her ailing mother, and her new identity as an ex-wife.

But Tim's affair has larger, more dangerous ramifications for the entire Knox family. The Knox children, Matthew and Laurel, are dealing with their parents' divorce in destructive ways. Matthew has become a wild-child, hanging out with a dangerous thief. Laurel cuts herself—both as a cry for help and a way to hurt her father. And Tim's new life with his mistress and her children isn't as fulfilling as he imagined it would be. He longs to return to his wife, children, and old life.

When his son goes missing under suspicious circumstances, Tim finds that longing fulfilled—though not in the way he had hoped. While the repercussions of his mistakes fill him with regret, it may be too late to alter the

Knoxs' tragic path—and his past may completely destroy the very thing Tim desperately needs: his family.

With an MFA in creative writing from Warren Wilson College, I have taught high school Japanese for ten years and English for twenty years. My work has been published in *Stickman Review, Crate, Primavera, Wild Violet,* and *Gulf Stream*. I attended the Bread Loaf Writers' Conference in 1999 and received an honorable mention in *Glimmer Train*'s July 2012 Very Short Fiction contest. I write using the pen name Telisha Moore Leigg.

Thank you for considering my completed 42,000-word novel.

Sincerely,

Sharon Leigg

How To Write A Query For An Essay Collection

Essay collections that offer vivid, larger-than-life stories of a person's true adventures can do quite well with literary agents and publishers. That said, getting your essay collection published won't necessarily be *easy*. To boost your chances for success, you've got to lay the groundwork to show there will be popular interest in your query.

If you haven't done so already, please go back and read the section about writing a query letter for a short story collection. Essay and short story collections benefit from similar strategies.

However, for an essay collection, it's what you've done in your life and how well you've told your story that will matter most. Essay collections from unpublished writers can do well if the writer's true stories have big appeal and are well crafted. Bonus points if you have a popular blog or some notoriety for your exploits.

Sample Query (Memoir)

This client gave her memoir a unique format by writing it as a series of related essays. Including the information that many of the essays have already been published in literary journals shows agents that there is already an audience interested in her story and her writing.

Dear Agent,

As a child growing up on a farm, I did my best to avoid gardening. But as an adult constantly learning to cultivate an intimate relationship with God, I began to view gardening as an outward reflection of my inner struggles and desires.

My book of spiritual essays, *A Garden Enclosed*, is an intimate look at my life as a Benedictine hermit and founder of Transfiguration Hermitage, a semi-eremitical community devoted to prayer and solitude. The hermit elders instructed me, "Sit in your cell and your cell will teach you everything." But I might amend their advice to say, "Sit in your garden."

My essays explore the issues of human life by looking at them through the lessons taught by gardening and nature: A falling tree represents the fear of vulnerability; a field of blueberries helps one find one's niche. In my inclusive message, the Scriptures mingle with T. S. Eliot, Isabel Allende, and John Lennon, thereby appealing to spiritual seekers of all traditions.

In addition to writing and teaching formation for the Hermitage community, I have taught spirituality both on the seminary level and in adult education, and serve as retreat leader, spiritual director, and formation director for my community.

I would love to share all or a portion of my collection with you upon request. Essays from this collection have found an enthusiastic audience with *Eclectica Magazine, Forge, GreenPrints, Gryffin, Schuylkill Valley Journal, Westview,* and *Willow Review*—which awarded me the Willow Review 2011 prize for nonfiction. I have also written for *Catholic Digest, Echoes of Maine, Review for Religious,* and *The Ellsworth American,* and produced book reviews for *Capital Weekly, Spiritual Life,* and *Town Line*. I am currently finishing an MA in theology at St. John's University School of Theology.

I believe this collection is the next step for my work. I hope you'll be in touch so we can explore a partnership.

Sincerely,

Sr. Elizabeth Wagner

How To Send A Revised Book To An Agent Who Has Already Seen It

As writers, our work is never done. Some of us will spend years working on a book, and then, finally—once we think it's finished—we'll submit it to a literary agent. But just because a book has been submitted doesn't necessarily mean it stops evolving.

Often—once a project has been rejected—a writer will revise and revise until he or she thinks the book is a more attractive project. Then, it's time to resubmit. But what's the right way to do it?

As with so many things related to the publishing business—there are no "one size fits all" answers to difficult questions. Always do your research, follow guidelines, be courteous, and trust your professional intuition.

How To Resubmit To A Literary Agent

If you've written a novel, memoir, or proposal for a nonfiction book, and you've already sent your project to a literary agent for representation, it's not "wrong" to submit your project again. There are a number of good reasons you might consider resubmitting a manuscript:

- You have significantly revised.

- The market has become more favorable to your book genre.

- You have built up your professional writing bio since the last submission was made.

- Your book has been nominated for an award or received some other significant accolade that indicates that your project appeals to readers.

- You have reworked your query letter to be a more accurate representation of your work. NOTE: We are NOT suggesting that resubmitting a series of revised queries to find one that works is a good idea. However, if your first attempt at a query letter was perhaps a bit amateurish, and you've since revised it, then you may be in a good position to resubmit.

THE BOTTOM LINE: If there is a reason that your book is more attractive now than it was ten years ago (or even ten months ago), then it may be worth your while to do another round of resubmissions.

How Long Should You Wait Before Resubmitting The Same Project To An Agent?

The answer to this question is a bit subjective. Obviously, it would not make sense to submit a project to a literary agent only a few weeks after that same project was rejected. A few months might be too short a time frame as well—but it depends on your particular circumstances and your correspondence with the agent in question.

If a literary agent requested revisions in your rejection letter, then you probably should not wait overly long to resubmit. Once the revisions are done, resubmit the project to the agent who offered you the critique. Be sure to clearly mark the envelope or subject line with "requested material."

Should You Mention That A Book Is Being Resubmitted In Your Query Letter?

If you had a personal conversation (via email or on the phone) with an agent about your project, then you may want to point out that your project is a revised resubmission. Or, if the agent had once requested sample pages and had already spent time reading the manuscript before, then it is worthwhile to let the agent know that the work has been substantially revised. Whatever the case, consider including the original correspondence if possible to jog the agent's memory about the conversation.

Otherwise, assuming that it has been at least a year since you started your revision, we recommend starting your resubmissions as if you're sending the book out for the first time. We see no compelling reason a writer should indicate "this book has already been around the block and had no takers, so I revised it."

Sample Query For A Revised Manuscript

This is a fictionalized letter to help you see what kinds of strategies can be used for a resubmission.

Dear Agent:

Twelve months ago you were kind enough to look at my completed 90,000-word thriller, *Dirt City*. Our original email correspondence is below. I found your feedback to be both helpful and inspiring, and with your notes in mind, I took a fresh look at the story.

Now, a year later, I'm resubmitting the revised version, and of course I thought of you because of your initial enthusiasm for the story. I'm willing to grant you a two-week exclusive look at the book before I start sending it off to other literary agencies for consideration.

Let me remind you of the story: In *Dirt City*, Rodney "Bolt" Dayton is the dirtiest of dirty cops: He takes bribes to ignore petty thefts, wheels and deals with lawmakers, and confiscates "job perks" from the evidence room. But when his ex-girlfriend's boss's daughter plays the damsel-in-distress card and begs him to find her missing boyfriend, Rodney reluctantly agrees to help. Unfortunately, the only way to find the kidnapped kid is to actually side with the "good guys" for once in his life. But will Rodney be able to stand the annoyances of being squeaky clean in order to help a girl he doesn't even like very much? And if not, then what's in it for him?

As for me, let me offer you my bio once again: I'm a former police officer turned professional dog trainer. I self-published my first book, *Dog Brain*, and received rave reviews from readers, bloggers, and reviewers alike (*Kirkus* said my book is "delightful and informative"). I also hit the Amazon best seller lists. When I'm not writing, I build model airplanes and practice martial arts. You can find out more about me at www.WritersWebsite.com.

If you would like a first look at *Dirt City*, please let me know as soon as you're able. Again, thanks for your kind words about the first draft of the book and for your nudge to tackle some revisions. The story has changed, but the heart of what you liked about it—Rodney's antihero antics—is even stronger than before.

Thank you for reconsidering this *Dirt City*.

Regards,

Joe P. Writer

Part Seven

Necessary Repairs: What To Do If Your Query Isn't Working

How To Regroup And Revise

Not Getting Results? How To Think Like An Agent

If your query letter isn't getting the results you want, it's time to start thinking like a literary agent. Although we at Writer's Relief are not literary agents, some staffers have had agency and publishing experience. Plus, we've been submitting our clients' work to literary agents since 1994, so we know what works.

Here are some of the questions that might cross an agent's mind when reading your query letter:

What's wrong with this book? Some agents will eyeball a query letter for red flags even before they thoroughly read it. It's only natural; skimming saves time. In an upcoming section, we'll review how agents might use red flags to eliminate your book before getting to the second paragraph of your query.

How quickly does this query get to the point? Agents are busy. And to say they get a lot of mail is an understatement. If, after a quick once-over, an agent decides to give your query letter a more thorough read, then you're in luck. Be sure your query is clear, direct, and specific. No wishy-washy or inflated language. No padding. Concise and compelling is the way to go.

Am I having a strong emotional reaction to this book? If a writer can tug an agent's heartstrings or get him or her revved up to read more, it's very likely a "Please send me the complete manuscript" note will follow. But writers need to be cautious in their query letters: Saying, "This book will tug your heartstrings" isn't the same thing as actually tugging them.

What's the hook? In general, literary agents are looking for the element of a book that makes it stand out, something to distinguish it from all other books. There are multitudes of unpublished books out there about lawyers who fight the good fight, personal assistants to the stars, women's friendships, jaded ex-investigators who have to save the world, well-intentioned books written by people who persevered through suffering… The list goes on. The reason there are so many books on familiar subjects is that there's a timelessness to certain stories. But what agents want to know is, "How is this book different?"

NOTE: A writer shouldn't spell out the reasons a book is different in the query letter; the thing that makes the book unique should be so clear and distinguishable that an agent won't need the book's X-factor pointed out.

Is it fresh? Some writers are able to ride the coattails of best sellers by writing books that echo popular themes and ideas (think of all the vampire books for teens that followed *Twilight*). But for the most part, new is better. Agents want to find the next big thing, not the last one.

Is this a promising, serious writer who has what it takes to write professionally? When an agent looks at a writer's bio, he or she wants to know: "Am I looking at an up-and-coming sensation?" When you publish your work in literary journals and magazines, you assert: "I know how this process works, I've weathered rejection, I'm a go-getter, I'm making connections, I'm a hard worker, and I'm in it for the long haul."

That said, agents have been known to take on authors who have no publishing credits at all. But having reputable literary journal credits in your bio can be a big help. If you don't have any, consider taking some time to build up your bio (and your experience).

Is it relevant? The stronger your book ties into the current trends and moods of the country (or the world), the better. But being trendy is not necessarily about artificially keying into a trend to exploit it; it's about being tuned in, authentic, and writing books that speak to the concerns of the moment. For some people, being tuned in means watching the nightly news and writing political stories. For others, it simply means deep, personal introspection about the human condition.

Every literary agency is different, and every agent is different.

The beauty of literary agencies is that they are diverse. At some agencies, queries are first vetted by junior agents or interns. At others, all queries are read by the agents they are sent to.

Some agents will skim. Others will read every word. Some will focus in on the commercial aspects of a query, and some won't think about that at all until well after emotional excitement has taken hold.

But while every agent is unique, many query readers consider at least some of the questions we've listed here. And they're good questions to put to your own query and book project. Good luck!

Red Flags: 6 Shortcuts Agents Will Use To Immediately Reject You

Everybody knows the best way to get an agent's attention is to write well and target submissions well. But did you ever stop to wonder what red flags professional readers look for when they're slogging through piles and piles of queries?

Think of it this way: When you're deciding whether or not you want to eat at a particular restaurant, you're going to glance at the menu quickly before you read the details about the individual appetizers, entrées, and desserts.

If you're a hard-core carnivore, you're probably going to pick out tofu, tempeh, and seitan as red flags. No need to spend any more time looking at this menu! We're off to the steak house!

The agents who are reading queries (until their eyes go blurry) also have shortcuts. They look for red flags that can mean "this might end up being a rejection."

Here at Writer's Relief, we are unable to accept every writer who wants to work with us. We typically turn away about 80 percent of writers who apply to join our client list. That means we read a lot of submissions. While we read absolutely every single submission that is sent to us—often with multiple readers—we (like literary agencies) *do* notice signs that suggest a writer may not be a good fit.

Here are the MOST COMMON red flags we see in our Review Board submissions:

1. Did not follow submission guidelines. When a writer's submission is way outside of our submission guidelines, he or she may be (inadvertently) proclaiming:

- I don't feel like following guidelines.
- I am not taking this seriously.
- I am not able to follow the directions (this could be for any number of reasons, some of which are legit).

Some red flags are like the miniature ones that children wave at parades. But blatantly ignoring submission guidelines is a red flag the size of a parachute. HINT: If you are going to break the "rules" when making a submission, it may help to explain in your query letter why you're doing it. Agents may be forgiving if they know what to forgive!

2. Formatting. Submit in a simple, common font with your name and page number on each page. The writing should stand out; the formatting should not.

3. Typos. Time and time again, we find typos—starting with the first line of the submission. Even if it's just an out-of-place comma, those little faux pas are annoying to a reader who still has ninety more submissions to get through. Sure, we'll forgive typos here and there. Nobody's prefect (did you catch it?)! But one can take only so many misspellings of the word "there" before the work screams "sloppy amateur!"

4. Project isn't suitable for submission. We've had people submit 385,000-word doorstops...er...novels, 50,000-word "short stories," and 150,000-word "novellas." Inappropriate word counts are not necessarily deal-breakers, but they are red flags.

5. Lack of supplemental materials. At Writer's Relief, we like to get a sense of a writer's personality because we need to work closely with our clients. We like to cultivate good energy here in our office, and we prefer to work with writers who are as enthusiastic about what they do as we are about helping them do it!

But some writers will fail to include a bio. Or they'll write "I'm a writer" and leave it at that. Imagine if you were interested in learning more about a writer's goals, interests, and history, but all he or she told you was "I like to write."

6. Writers who send us long, bitter diatribes. We see a number of writers who complain about how literary agents won't take them seriously, about how nobody understands, about how somebody who helped them self-publish a project ripped them off and now is entirely to blame for the failure of the book.

We get it; publishing is a tough biz. ALL writers have it tough at some point. It's the ones who don't consider themselves victims who persevere and succeed.

The Red Flags Exception

It rarely happens, but sometimes we come across a truly great writer who made errors when submitting. Or we find a submission that is so compelling, the writer could have submitted in crayon and we wouldn't care. (NOTE: This

Necessary Repairs: What To Do If Your Query Isn't Working

is an imaginary scenario. We do not accept submissions in crayon—at least not from anyone over the age of three.)

The point is this: If you want to increase your chances of getting an acceptance letter, consider the way that literary agents might use shortcuts to weed through submissions. Then, avoid hoisting those red flags.

11 Common Query Letter Mistakes

To recap—here are the eleven most common mistakes we see in query letters.

Cheesy lead. Don't be cute. Skip the rhetorical questions. The "What if you were stuck on a sailboat in a hurricane with a mysterious killer?" teasers get old fast. Better to lead with the story; otherwise, your reader may feel as if you're trying to manipulate him or her to create more sensation than your book warrants.

Bobbled blurbs. The biggest problems we see with blurbs are: 1) too many characters and secondary characters mentioned when only the main character should be the emotional hook; 2) a description that's more thematic than plot-driven (for example, "this book is about peace and love"); and 3) the author attempts to tell the whole story, including the ending, when he or she should use the blurb as a teaser instead.

Appearance. The letter looks bad, smells, is printed on cheap paper or photocopied, etc. We also receive electronic queries that are poorly formatted; all caps, multiple colors and silly fonts, goofy pictures in the signature line, etc. Or the letter loses its formatting once it's sent. TIP: Test your e-query to make sure it keeps its formatting by sending it to your family members and friends to see what it looks like in their in-boxes. Then you can send it to agents.

Mentioning prior manuscripts (and/or certain self-published books). Go back and read our section entitled "How And When To Mention Multiple Books (Or A Series) In A Query Letter."

The multiple-personality bio. Often writers begin their bios in first person, but wind up in third. Be on the lookout for pronouns gone wild! Also, some bios will begin in present tense, but then end in past.

Groveling. It may seem like it makes sense to acknowledge your own humility by pointing out a lack of experience, but resist this urge. Confidence earns respect.

TMI. While it's always good to convey your own unique personality in your bio, be careful not to include *too much information*. If your novel is about sailors, it may help to include your background in the Coast Guard. Be personable and interesting but do so with care.

Listing publishing credits that aren't really publishing credits. Be careful that the publishing credentials you're listing are not part of poetry-contest scams or anthology scams. Including bad credits suggests you don't know the market and may be too much of a newbie to write well.

Copyright. Industry standard is to not include the copyright symbol on your work.

Cover art. If you include cover art, you show: a) that you don't know how the industry works (since writers get almost no say over their covers) and b) that you might just be the kind of high-maintenance writer who wants complete control.

If you flatter, mean it. Agents can see straight through the "I greatly admire your agency" bit; they know a generic form letter compliment when they see one. If you're going to offer flattery, be specific in your praise.

6 Sentences That Should Never Appear In Your Query

This is the first book I've ever written! It may be true, but don't say it; this won't be considered a positive point by the agent.

I've been writing since I was five. Writers who feel compelled to explain that "I've been writing since I was X years old" or that "It is my greatest wish to get published" inadvertently declare to agents, "I am a newbie."

This would make a great movie. Almost everyone thinks his or her book could be a great movie. You want your query letter to ask your agent to do one thing and one thing only: represent and sell your BOOK—not a screenplay, not a series of action figures, not your foreign rights. Let the agent decide if your book is screen-worthy or not.

This book will appeal to readers of all genres. Literary agents want to work with writers who understand that each genre appeals to a very specific demographic. When you say, "This appeals to everyone," an agent will read, "This appeals to no one in particular."

My friends/parents/teachers like my writing. New writers almost always get favorable responses to their writing from loved ones. But unless your mom or dad is a renowned literary critic, leave off any amateur praise.

My book is the next *Harry Potter*. If the story is solid and the writing is strong, there's no reason an author should feel obligated to proclaim that a book is the next big seller. Don't promise what you have no control over. Let your work speak for itself.

Necessary Repairs: What To Do If Your Query Isn't Working

Example Of A Very Bad Query Letter (Just For Fun)

Dear Sir and/or Madam:

Are you ready to have you're mind blown?

Please find enclosed my entire 300,000-word erotic romance thriller novel, *The Tale of Blah*, the first part of a five-book series based on events in my own life.

Have you ever wondered what it's like to rule the world? When the main character, Bob, wakes up after a bender in Las Vegas, he finds himself in the White House as the President of Earth. Bob is short and fat with thinning hair. He has a best friend named Bart whose wife Candy is the sister of the owner of an evil corporation named Jeff.

This book starts off slow, but really picks up around the third chapter. Members of my prison writing group really liked it. Together, we could sell millions of copies to fans of Harry Potter, *Catcher in the Rye*, and the Bible.

Please call me with your thoughts. As this is a top secret project, this is the only copy, so please return it with the contract ASAP. Also, I've already copyrighted the book so you can't steal my ideas.

Let's make some money,

Annoying L. Person

Are you done smacking yourself on the forehead? Good. Now let's go back and examine exactly why this query letter is so very, very bad.

"Dear Sir and/or Madam:"

Other than implying gender confusion on the agent's part, this shows that Annoying L. Person didn't take the time to research the name of the agent he or she is querying. If you are querying an agency that doesn't mention the specific names of its agents, use a generic salutation: "Dear Literary Agent."

"Are you ready to have you're mind blown?"

If you can't tell why opening your letter with something like this is a huge no-no, you might be beyond our help. Not only is there a glaring error (you're instead of your), but the lead is needy and bombastic.

"Please find enclosed my entire 300,000-word erotic romance adventure thriller novel, *The Tale of Blah*, the first part of a five-book series based on events in my own life."

First, most novels top out at 100,000 words. And even if you can pull off a ridiculously long book, sending the whole manuscript without an invitation to do so is bonkers. There's a reason submission guidelines exist.

Second, while it's common for contemporary novels to be a hybrid of multiple genres, you don't want to write yourself into a corner that doesn't appeal to the fans of any genre involved. And you should just focus on the specific book at hand. An agent can only take on one project at a time—it doesn't make sense to try to sell Book Two unless you can sell Book One.

"Have you ever wondered what it's like to rule the world?"

Now we're up to two rhetorical questions, both of which are way too cliché.

"When the main character, Bob, wakes up after a bender in Las Vegas, he finds himself in the White House as the President of Earth. Bob is short and fat with thinning hair. He has a best friend named Bart whose wife Candy is the sister of the owner of an evil corporation named Jeff."

Where do we even begin? Ignoring the fact that this too-brief synopsis tells nothing of what actually happens in the book, it's full of too many secondary characters (including the "evil corporation named Jeff"). You should mention only the main character (without having to identify him or her as such) and bring up other characters only if they are integral to the story.

"This book starts off slow, but really picks up around the third chapter. Members of my prison writing group really liked it. Together, we could sell millions of copies to fans of Harry Potter, *Catcher in the Rye*, and the Bible."

We say this often, but it bears repeating: Write a story that starts with a bang! Don't make someone wait three chapters to see things heat up, especially considering that most agents only want to see the first few pages. And while

Necessary Repairs: What To Do If Your Query Isn't Working

it's great that your prison writing group really liked it, they probably have no clout in the industry: The agent's response will likely be a big "Who cares?"

Sometimes it can help to draw comparisons to other books in the same genre—but unless the comparisons are careful and strategic, it can come across as cocky—almost as presumptuous as the assumption that the book will definitely "sell millions of copies."

Be realistic in your query letter! And: Don't. Mention. Harry. Potter. The chances are pretty good that every agent has heard this over and over again, ad nauseam.

"[Insert writer bio here]"

You'll notice that this writer offers no biographical information whatsoever. In a best-case scenario, a writer will have at least some writing credits or can demonstrate a commitment to craft.

"Please call me with your thoughts. As this is a top secret project, this is the only copy, so please return it with the contract ASAP. Also, I've already copyrighted the book so you can't steal my ideas."

It's a bit silly to assume an agent will call you (generally, they shy away from phone calls to anyone but clients). And—ignoring the fact that you should never send your whole manuscript—make sure whatever you send isn't the only copy! Any number of bad things can happen to pages in the mail. Plus, good agents are NOT out to steal your manuscript or your ideas. As long as you're submitting to *reputable* agencies, you're okay.

"Let's make some money,"

What are the chances this phrase was the prelude to our imaginary Annoying L. Person's prison stint?

Part Eight

Query Letter Checklists

Checklists For Your Query Letter

PRINT QUERY LETTER CHECKLIST

DO:

- Include an SASE with every postal submission. Send only a business-size envelope with postage.
- Define the genre of your submission and give an accurate word count.
- Proofread carefully.
- Double-check spelling—especially of the agent's name—and verify the addresses.
- Demonstrate enthusiasm for your project.
- Include your current contact information.
- Focus on the appearance of the query: use 8½- by 11-inch, high-quality bond letterhead, and print using a high-quality printer.
- Include any enclosures promised in the query.
- Send only one project per agent at a time.
- Weed out all irrelevant information or material.
- Do your best to comply with requests from literary agents. If you're difficult to work with, an agent won't want to sign a contract with you.

DO NOT:

- Exceed the one-page limit!
- Ask that your synopsis or sample pages be returned.
- Bind your manuscript in any way (no staples or clips).
- Force an agent to sign for your package.
- Send your only copy of the materials.
- Send work from the *middle* of your novel or memoir.
- Annoy agents by calling or emailing them to verify they received your package.
- Send a coffee-stained query with multiple typos or crossed-out words.
- Query with an incomplete novel or memoir.
- Disregard agency guidelines.
- Make threats, as in "*If I don't hear from you in six weeks, I'll submit elsewhere.*"
- Send the same project to multiple in-house agents at the same agency

simultaneously.
- Call and complain if a project is rejected.
- Disrespect the receptionist, editorial assistant, or any other member of the house staff.
- Mention fees, budget, or compensation.
- Send a multiple-choice postcard where an editor can check a box if he or she is interested.
- Send material that is irrelevant.

E-QUERY LETTER CHECKLIST

- Your e-query meets all the expectations for a print query as stated in the prior section.
- Your e-query is written in a clear, easy-to-read font. (Don't use colors.)
- Keep your e-query short and concise.
- The subject header is clear and stated as the agent requests. (For example: Query—Science-Fiction Novel by Name.)
- You left out any signature quotes, emoticons, clip art.
- Your email address is professional.
- You thoroughly read the guidelines regarding attachments.
- Retain a copy of your query for your records.
- Send yourself (and your friends) a test copy to check the formatting.

Part Nine

More Sample Query Letters

More Sample Query Letters! Compare And Contrast

We thought it might be instructive to examine a single book idea from multiple perspectives in order to shine a light on the differences that arise when you switch from one genre to another in a query.

So in the following pages, we take an imaginary book called *Fowl Play* across multiple genres. We hope you'll find it helpful to see how the letter changes from one genre/angle to another!

Fowl Play **- The Novel**

Dear Agent First and Last Name:

I would like you to consider my 65,000-word amateur-sleuth mystery novel, *Fowl Play*, for representation.

Jennie Jorgensen is a dedicated chicken breeder who regularly shows her unusual, prizewinning poultry at national competitions. When her former colleague Bess Bluefoot goes missing, Jennie finds herself drawn into the mystery by Bess's good-looking brother, Tom Turnkey.

As Jennie gets to know Tom, she suddenly finds that her perfectly pristine flock of hens is under investigation by the National Board of Show Fowl. And she begins to wonder if Bess's disappearance isn't tied into whisperings of a scandal involving genetically modified pullets. As the mystery gets deeper, so does Jennie's relationship with Tom. But can they find Bess before it's too late?

Before moving to the city, I spent a decade in Latin America raising chickens. My poetry has appeared in the *Latin America Press* and *Wind Five Folded*, and my stories have appeared or are forthcoming in *Mangrove*, *Post Road*, and *The MacGuffin*. I am active on Facebook, and you can find me and my 10,000 followers at @ChickForBrains on Twitter. My website is www.FowlPlay.com.

Thank you for your time. I have attached a synopsis and sample pages for your convenience.

Sincerely,

Your Name
Street Address
City, State Zip
Phone Number
Email Address

Fowl Play - **The Memoir**

Dear Agent First and Last Name:

Please consider my 90,000-word memoir, *Fowl Play*, for representation.

I was a dedicated chicken breeder for twenty years, and I regularly showed my unusual, prizewinning poultry at national competitions. I was known around the world for my exceptional roosters and at one point was featured in *The New York Times* and on the television show *Backyard Homesteading*. I've written many articles for industry trade magazines as well as mainstream magazines like *Esquire* and *Woman's Day*.

I loved my life as a breeder—until the day my colleague Bess Bluefoot went missing. When the local police brushed off the case, I decided to investigate.

My search for Bess led me deep into a world of blackmail and high-stakes scandals surrounding the chicken-breeding industry. Along the way, I came to rely on Bess's brother, Tom, for information and support, and eventually we fell in love. I began to suspect that Bess's disappearance was tied into a cover-up involving genetically modified pullets. But when we finally did find Bess, we discovered secrets about the poultry business and the U.S. government that shocked me—including a system of breeding poultry that resulted in odd birds that barely resembled "chickens" as we know them.

It's my hope that sharing my story will shed much-needed light on an important element of the food industry that not many people are aware of. To my knowledge, no one has ever approached this topic in book form before.

My poetry has appeared in the *Latin America Press* and *Wind Five Folded*, and my stories have appeared or are forthcoming in *Mangrove, Post Road*, and *The MacGuffin*. I am active on Facebook, and you can find me and my 10,000 followers at @ChickForBrains on Twitter. My website is www.FowlPlay.com.

Thank you for your time. I have attached a synopsis and sample pages for your convenience.

Sincerely,

Your Name
Street Address
City, State Zip
Phone Number
Email Address

Fowl Play - **The How-To Book**

Dear Agent First and Last Name:

Please consider my 100,000-word book, *Fowl Play*, which teaches urban homesteaders how to create rooftop henhouses on city buildings.

Fowl Play offers simple solutions for urban dwellers who want to get in on the homesteading craze that's sweeping the nation. A recent surge in interest about chickens has been cataloged in articles found in journals from *Redbook* to *Sunday Morning*. People are actively looking for resources to help them engage in environmentally friendly, modern homesteading practices. My book draws on my expertise and shares practical tips and strategies for keeping chickens for meat, eggs, and show.

I delve into topics such as:

- Chicken breeds and their special characteristics
- Raising healthy chickens
- Chicken folklore and fun facts
- How to build a henhouse
- Selling your eggs

Fowl Play has been endorsed by the Chicken Farmers of America. And [famous celebrity] has offered to blurb the book if it finds publication.

I was a dedicated chicken breeder for twenty years and I regularly showed my unusual, prizewinning poultry at national competitions. I was known around the world for my exceptional roosters, and at one point was featured in *The New York Times* and on the television show *Backyard Homesteading*. I've written many articles about chickens for industry trade magazines as well as mainstream magazines like *Esquire* and *Woman's Day*. I am active on Facebook, and you can find me and my 10,000 followers at @ChickForBrains on Twitter. My website is www.FowlPlay.com.

Thank you for your time. Please allow me to send over my complete proposal if you're interested!

Sincerely,

Your Name
Street Address
City, State Zip
Phone Number
Email Address

More Sample Query Letters

Fowl Play - As Popular Nonfiction

Dear Agent First and Last Name:

"Acting like a chicken" usually means being a wimp. But in truth, chickens are anything but cowards! As the trend of urban homesteaders booms and chicken supplies sales soar, my book *Fowl Play; For the Love of Chickens* gives animal lovers a look into the secret life of chickens and their human keepers.

All over the country, homesteaders and homesteader aficionados are clamoring to know more about chickens, and my humorous book is chock-full of trivia, tips, and folklore. Chickens are fascinating from the moment they're born—and I'm not even talking about the old chicken-or-the-egg question. The egg is an incredible miracle of evolutionary design—it can withstand over fifty pounds of pressure, but can be cracked by a newborn chick. And why not? Baby chickens are the closest living relatives to Tyrannosaurs—think of that the next time you see a fluffy, little yellow chick!

Sections of my book focus on various chicken-related phenomena: words derived from life with chickens; the relatively new problem of "stray" chickens in cities; the environmental impact of chickens; and—yes—some recipes.

Major Magazine said, "The number of people raising chickens has increased XXX percent in three years." Part history, part science, and part pop culture, *Fowl Play* speaks to chicken lovers everywhere. If you don't already adore chickens, you will once you've read this book. Chickens are really amazing. But no one has published a fun, easy-to-read book yet for chicken lovers. It's time we corrected that!

Fowl Play has been endorsed by the Chicken Farmers of America. And [famous celebrity] has offered to blurb the book if it finds publication.

I was a dedicated chicken breeder for twenty years, and I regularly showed my unusual, prizewinning poultry at national competitions. I was known around the world for my exceptional roosters and at one point was featured in *The New York Times* and on the television show *Backyard Homesteading*. I've written many articles about chickens for industry trade magazines as well as mainstream magazines like *Esquire* and *Woman's Day*. I am active on Facebook, and you can find me and my 10,000 followers at @ChickForBrains on Twitter. My website is www.FowlPlay.com.

Thank you for your time. Please allow me to send over my complete proposal if you're interested!

Sincerely,

Your Name
Street Address
City, State Zip
Phone Number
Email Address

Bonus Section

- **What's The Purpose Of A Cover Letter**
- **Getting A Quote From A Famous Author**
- **Making Submissions To Literary Journals Via A Submission Manager**
- **Signs Of A Healthy Submission Strategy**
- **How To Stay Motivated**
- **Getting Help**
- **Free Resources**

What's The Purpose Of A Cover Letter?

A cover letter is sent to a literary journal or magazine and contains basic information about a writer's submitted material and a professional bio. It's not a sales pitch. Not a plea for attention. It's just a "what" and "by who" introduction with some industry etiquette added for good measure.

Why isn't a cover letter a sales pitch? Simple. Most staffers at literary magazines are volunteers who take deep pride in the fact that every single submission receives serious consideration—sometimes from multiple readers. There's little or no money involved; it's all love.

Sure, there are probably *some* editors in the world who are picky about what they're even willing to consider. But in our experience, those folks are the exception to the rule. If you send a submission to a reputable lit mag, it's going to be read. In fact, some literary journal volunteers won't even look at your cover letter until *after* they've read the submission so that they won't be prejudiced by anything said in the letter itself.

The good people at *The Review Review,* a literary journal that draws its contents from other literary journals, conducted interviews with editors and former editors to get the real scoop on cover letters. Their findings are fascinating, ranging from "cover letters are important" to "cover letters don't matter at all."

Here are a few of the editor's responses:

Actual Editor Opinions On Cover Letters

Karen Rile, writer and editor of *Cleaver* Magazine:
It helps us pick a mix of established and emerging writers. For example, it helps to know when a submitter is still in high school or college. We read the letters after we read the submission; however…when a writer simply types "I prefer to let my work speak for myself" or something to that nature in the cover letter section (we also require a cover letter), it strikes me as a little off. We won't disregard their work, and if it truly speaks well for itself, we'll still take it. But I'm not going out of my way to accept a submission from an author who seems like s/he might be difficult to deal with.

Sean Thomas Dougherty, poet and former editor:
Not very. I don't think we really looked at them.

RW Spryszak, writer and editor of *Thrice Fiction*:
Thrice Fiction magazine has a distinct policy on that. We don't read them, and we even ask submitters not to bother (not that everybody reads the guidelines, however). Our reasoning is pretty straightforward. On the one hand, we want to keep the work as "the thing," and consequently we've published a hefty number of first-time authors. Meaning never appeared anywhere before. On the other hand, we don't want to be swayed by a writer's rep.

Josh Medsker, writer and editor of *Twenty-Four Hours Zine*:
They are important because they help determine whether the writer has read the magazine's submission guidelines.

Calvin Hennick, writer and former editor:
I helped edit a lit mag that struggled to get quality submissions, and so mentions of previous publications and MFA programs earned a slightly closer read if we happened to look at the cover letter. But we didn't always look, and again, the advantage was slight.

Catherine Elcik, writer and fiction editor of *The Drum*:
I ignore them until after I'm invested in the story.

Barbara Diehl, writer and editor of *The Baltimore Review*:
Bottom line: Not important. The work is what matters.

Thomas Dodson, writer and editor of *Printer's Devil Review*:
The editors will likely be interested to know where else you've had work published and if you chose to submit to their magazine in particular for some reason. Beyond that, my advice would be to observe the principle of non-maleficence [sic]: first, do no harm. The work itself is what matters, so just don't do anything in the cover letter that is likely to throw up a red flag.

Deirdra McAfee, writer and former editor:
Why not take a lousy minute or two to present yourself well too. Show you take yourself seriously as a writer and that the journal matters to you—that's the ticket.

Michael Nye, writer and editor of *The Missouri Review*:
We encourage staff to read the work first, the letter second, if at all. Loosely, they do not matter. However, two exceptions. First, if you're an unpublished writer. *TMR*, and all lit mags, love being a first publication for an unpublished writer, and the only way we would know that is through the cover letter. Second, if your cover letter has LOLcats or is fifteen pages long or whatnot, and screams "I am an insane person!" then we notice that too.

So, practically speaking, what does all of this mean to your cover letter writing?

For the most part, your cover letter doesn't have to be wildly clever, attention-grabbing, or flashy. It just has to be professional and demonstrate a knowledge of the publishing industry.

Also, since someone is going to read your submission no matter what, your cover letter does NOT need to give a summary or explanation of the submitted material. Really. It doesn't. Resist the urge to explain.

By explaining your plot or motifs, you might inadvertently imply that you suspect the editor at a lit mag must be *lured* into reading your submission. Also, explaining a story, poem, or essay in a cover letter basically tells the editor that you think he or she is not intelligent enough to figure out the plot and themes on his or her own.

Sometimes submission guidelines indicate that the editors *want* you to provide a bit of atypical information in your cover letter—in that case, feel free to oblige. But otherwise, leave out any explanations of your story, themes, or ideas. Stick to the basics.

Basic Cover Letter Elements

After your salutation, it's time to get down to business. In one sentence, let the literary editor know what you're submitting.

For cover letters, this is a pretty simple process.

For short prose submitted to literary journals:

- Attached please find my 2,000-word short story, "The Marriage," for your consideration.
- Please consider my 2,500-word essay, "On My Mother's Knee."
- Enclosed please find my 3,500-word mixed genre piece, "The Author's First Rodeo."

Notice: Each of the above examples gives a word count, and the titles are in quotes.

For poetry submitted to literary journals:

For poetry, you can choose how to organize your titles:

- Please consider my attached poems: *Fishing; On the Old Cliffs; Mr. Shriner's Dog;* and *Marking Time.*

Or

- Please consider my enclosed poems:

    "Fishing"
    "On the Old Cliffs"
    "Mr. Shriner's Dog"
    "Marking Time"

Notice: You do not need to include the line count of your poems.

Then include your bio information. Your bio for a cover letter is the same as what you would write for a query letter. See the previous section on query letters, "Element #4: Your Author Bio: Make A Great Impression!"

Your closing line for a cover letter is also similar to a query letter. Review the query letter section titled "Element #5: Knowing How To Say Goodbye."

How To Ask A Famous Author For A Quote

Call it what you like: a book blurb, a cover quote, an endorsement...whatever the name, it can take a lot of courage and tenacity to ask a famous (or even semi-famous) author for a quote for your writing—whether you're a new writer or a veteran.

Many writers are able to use their connections to procure endorsements to include in their cover or query letters. But before you start sending out emails willy-nilly to your favorite writers asking them to write a quote for you, it's important to know the etiquette.

How To Request A Quote From An Author

Prepare in advance for the day you'll need a quote. The best time to start looking for the perfect person to blurb your writing is BEFORE you need it. NOW is a good time to start laying the groundwork for getting a successful book blurb in the future. You don't want to ask an author you don't personally know for a quote, but you might feel comfortable asking for a blurb from a writer you've met at a networking event.

Generally, authors who request a blurb BEFORE they have a publishing deal must restrict their requests to writers they personally know. Some of our clients have asked their well-known professors or members of their writing groups for quotes. To meet other writers, join trade organizations in your genre. Take classes. Go to readings. Even if you don't end up rubbing elbows with too many best sellers, you never know who your friends know. Personal connections always trump cold calls and out-of-the-blue requests. So get out there and shake some hands!

Make friends on social media. If you can't establish any personal connections, turn to social media. Don't pop onto an author's Facebook page and start asking for favors. Instead, just show yourself as the likable, interested/interesting author that you are. Once you've established a genuine rapport and connection with the author, you may be more comfortable asking for a quote.

Ask nicely in a well-composed, personal email. Don't send your request by Facebook or Twitter; email is best, when possible. Here are the salient points to include in your letter asking for a book quote:

- Introduce yourself in a personal way, then mention you're asking for a cover quote.

- Include a reminder of how you know/where you met the author. Are you in the same writing group? Did you speak to him or her at a writing conference?

- If you're requesting a book endorsement, briefly offer details: genre, story, publisher, release date (if any).

- Specifically say why you think the author in question is a kindred spirit who might like your writing (Because you also like his/her writing? Because one of the author's titles compares well with yours? Because you both love and write about Dalmatians? Because you both like lighthearted adventures?).

- Give the author a deadline for the potential endorsement, but offer as big a timeline as possible.

- Let the author know where the blurb will be used. Your book cover? Your author website? Your cover or query letter?

- Say thank you!

Book Endorsement Etiquette

Generally speaking, you should never have to pay for a book endorsement. If you ask for a blurb, and an author gives you one, be sure to use it. If you don't like the whole quote, you're welcome to cherry-pick the phrases you like best (this is common publishing industry procedure).

Then, return the favor by promoting the author's books on your own social media pages. You might even want to send a thank-you gift. And remember, later on down the line when a new writer asks *you* for a book blurb, pass the favor along and write the book blurb.

Following is a sample letter to use as an example if you are writing a letter to an author to request a quote, endorsement, or blurb for your own book.

We've written this letter from the perspective of an unpublished writer who has a manuscript ready to send to agents (like you!), and who wants to ask a fellow writer for a quote. But you can use the same ideas even if you are asking for an endorsement for a cover letter. Just know that quotes in query letters are far more helpful than quotes in cover letters. For more on why this is, read the bonus section titled: "What's The Purpose Of A Cover Letter?"

We don't recommend using this sample letter as a template: it's important that your letter asking for a book endorsement is truly heartfelt and personal. But seeing an example will help you write your own quote request.

Bonus Section

Sample Letter For Requesting An Endorsement Quote

Dear Name of Colleague, Friend, or Fellow Writer,

This is (My Name) from (Organization That We're Both In). First, let me thank you in advance for reading my email! You know I've been at our meetings talking about the manuscript I've been working on. Well, after two years, it's done!

I'm now getting ready to send my manuscript out to literary agents for possible representation. But before I do, I wanted to ask if you might consider reading some or all of it, as your schedule allows? I don't need a critique, but if you feel the book has some merit, perhaps you'll feel comfortable saying a few words about it that I might include in my queries to literary agents (and that might possibly be included if the book's published).

I know it's a lot to ask! You've been so busy with XYZ… If you can't do it, don't worry! You know you'll continue to have my support as a fellow writer and fan!

Here's a brief overview of my book: *A Stone In Time* is about an Irish shepherdess who is transported to 2045—only to discover that she has been summoned as the last of her now-extinct bloodline to hunt down a tribe of murderous demons. She has to save the future to save her past.

I think you might like *A Stone In Time* because you and I are both writing time-travel science fiction—and we both love surprising plot lines and strong female characters.

[Alternative: I self-published my novel *A Stone In Time* last year and have been absolutely overwhelmed by the positive response. I hit the Amazon Best Seller lists within three months, and sales have been rising ever since. Now I'm transitioning into traditional publishing. And I would love to include an endorsement by my favorite author in my query letter and in future promotional efforts.] Note: *In this alternative, the writer can't guarantee that the endorsement will appear on a future cover, since only the future publisher could guarantee that. But the lure of getting a name out before a big fan base for a self-published book might be enough of a carrot to encourage another writer to offer a blurb.*

If you think you might be able to write a few words about my book, will you kindly give me an idea of when you might be able to respond? I'll hold off sending my queries until I hear from you one way or another.

Thanks so much for your consideration. It's been great getting to know you at ZYX, and it would be a true thrill and honor if you considered my book.

Sincerely,

Name

Following Up On Your Book Quote Request Email

If you don't hear back from an author you have contacted about a quote request, there are two possibilities: Either the author doesn't want to—or simply can't—offer a quote; or the author didn't get your email. We recommend that you follow up only once (with the text of your original email pasted at the bottom of the follow-up). Then, if you still don't get a response, it may be the author is too busy to offer you a quote, and it's time to look elsewhere.

15 Tricks That Will Make Your Life Easier When You Use A Submission Manager

Using an online submission form (or submission manager) is a very efficient way to submit your short stories, personal essays, and poetry to literary journals and magazines.

A submission manager is an online form (created by the recipient of your submission) that a writer fills out. The form creates a profile so that the writer can log in at any time to check on the status of a submission or make a change/update. When you use a submission manager, you won't necessarily need to send a cover or query letter in its traditional format. But you will need to have the *parts* of a traditional letter ready to be cut and pasted into a submission form.

There are some very specific things you can do to make your online submissions go more smoothly when using electronic submission managers.

Tips for Making Electronic Submissions to Literary Journals and Magazines

1. Keep track of which journals and editors you submit work to; the submission method that was used; and your user name/email address and password. Save this information where you can easily find it. This record keeping will save you a lot of time and frustration when you're trying to remember where you sent your submissions.

2. Use the same password each time so you don't have too many to remember. But don't use a password that you share with banks or email accounts or any other websites. Make one up specifically for your writing.

3. Create a new email address to use just for your e-subs (electronic submissions), or create folders in your email account to sort your acceptances and rejections.

4. Make sure you read each literary journal's submission guidelines carefully *before* you upload your manuscript! For example, some literary journals won't take work if your name appears on it.

5. Make sure your submission information is up to date. Literary journals change their online forms and submission managers from time to time. This could be the case if you find their usual submission link fails to load.

6. Submit to a group of journals that use Submittable (a specific online submission manager preferred by many lit mags). If you create an account with one journal that uses Submittable, you can use the same account for every journal that uses it. You'll also remain logged in to your account if you have cookies enabled on your computer. This will make it easy to fill out forms.

7. Have your cover letter or professional writing bio ready, because you'll be copying and pasting it into each submission. And remove any references to enclosures or attachments.

8. If submitting a group of poems, have a list of all the titles ready; you can copy and paste that into the forms and submission managers. Also, combine all of your poems into one file in case the submission manager only allows one file to be attached.

9. If you made a mistake on your submission while using an online form or submission manager, odds are you can log in to your account, withdraw your submission, and resubmit it. If the "oops" in question was in an email submission, you can try resending, but this might annoy editors who don't want duplicate emails. Hooray for submission managers!

10. Double-check your email addresses and URLs. The easiest e-sub mistake to make is a typo in the email address (or URL).

11. Keep a master electronic file of your work—and don't save any changes you make. If you need to tailor your work to a specific journal (i.e., no name on the work, single-spaced, no headers or footers, etc.), always save it as a new document. Having the original version to work with will save you a lot of time when you want to submit to another journal.

12. Don't save over the master version of your cover letter! (See Tip #11.)

13. You will most likely get an automatic response from an editor stating that they have received your work. Note: This is NOT a rejection. Carefully read your responses to avoid confusion. If the journal emailed you your account information, save this in a designated email folder.

14. Some journals require payment for sending an electronic submission. We don't discourage you from submitting to those journals; just make sure you include payment so your submission isn't rejected out of hand.

15. Make sure the literary journal is actually accepting the genre of work you are submitting. Sometimes a literary magazine can be closed for poetry but will still accept short stories.

The 7 Signs Of A Healthy Submission Strategy

How many of these seven signs of success are showing up in your writing life?

Your work is strong. You've done your homework. You read regularly and voraciously. You've spent your time in workshops, lectures, and writing conference seminars. You accept both praise and criticism. You have a sense of confidence in your writing—and it shows.

You know the drill. Along with mastering your craft, you've learned the publishing industry etiquette for submitting to literary agents or to literary journals. You know the proper format for a manuscript. You know the importance of professional proofreading. You know what your query letter or cover letter should say. Your submission packets and electronic submissions are polished, professional, and attractive.

You're submitting regularly and writing regularly. You take your submissions as seriously as you take your writing, and you're setting aside a time for both at regular intervals. Because your submissions are going out regularly, you're in a better position to get more publication offers and acceptance letters.

You look at rejection letters positively. You no longer feel a debilitating pang of disappointment when your work is turned down. You look at your rejection letters as badges of honor: They mean you're not letting the realities of the publishing industry get you down. You're out there; you're trying; you're a positive thinker.

You're not afraid of the numbers. Along with being positive about your rejection letters, you've also made it past the urge to "just quit" after a few submissions. You understand that submissions are, to some extent, a numbers game. You know that if a work is reasonably strong, there absolutely is somebody out there who wants to read it. And that means you're persistent. You'll send a given piece out for as long as it takes until it finds a good home.

You're getting better at knowing where NOT to send your work. In the beginning, you might have sent your writing almost everywhere. Now you're being more selective. You're spending more time researching literary journals and literary agents to find those best suited to your writing style.

You're striving to improve. Your writing is getting better. Your submissions are more targeted. Each day, you're pushing yourself to be the best you can be. And every time you think you've made it to the top, you discover an exciting new peak to climb. But you're in it, first and foremost, for the joy of the journey, not just the accolades.

Does This Sound Like You?

If so, congratulations! You've got a healthy submission strategy and the mindset to go the distance.

But if you're feeling frustrated, pessimistic, or just too busy to carve out the time needed to develop a strong submission strategy, it may be time to contact Writer's Relief. Our submission strategists are more than trained motivators who are there to keep you writing; they're also trained professionals who will regularly and expertly guide your submissions into the right hands.

How To Stay Motivated When You Want To Quit

Let's say you've developed the perfect submission strategy: You have a plan; you have all the know-how you need; and you have some really great writing to submit. If you're like many writers, you'll dive into your new submission strategy with all your enthusiasm and gumption.

But soon, your interest in making submissions may begin to fade. Before you know it, you're back to wondering why you never send out submissions to agents and editors. You know you should be making submissions—but you just don't.

Even the best submission strategy in the world is worthless if there is no motivation backing it up. Here is what you can do to stay focused and enthusiastic about implementing your personal submission strategy.

Keep your eye on the prize. There are many ways you can stay focused on your dreams: Post inspirational quotes in your home office. Buy yourself a trophy or some other meaningful item and set it next to your computer to remind yourself that your goal is a real, tangible thing. Do what you can to stay focused on what you want to achieve, and you will be more enthusiastic while getting there.

Reward yourself for success. If you set goals for yourself like, "I will make six submissions this week," then reward yourself when you meet that goal. Just make sure the reward is something you really want and something you would not otherwise allow yourself to have. Otherwise, a reward system will not work.

Seek out others who are in the same boat. When you're struggling, talking about your experiences can be a great way to stay motivated. It helps to vent, compare notes, and commiserate. Find the emotional support that you need to keep going. Hint: You can meet other writers at local writing groups, at writing organizations, or on the Web. You can find a comprehensive list of writing groups on our website.

Don't be too hard on yourself. At some point, everyone drops the ball. If you fall off the wagon, you can always climb back on. Don't let negativity hold you back—leave your mistakes behind you and move forward.

Don't procrastinate. Procrastination can trigger a vicious cycle: You put the work off because you don't feel like doing it; then you feel bad because you're not doing it, so you procrastinate some more. If you find yourself wanting to procrastinate, remind yourself of your goals. Focus on the end result, not on the work of getting there.

Find inspiration. Maybe reading books by your favorite author motivates you to work harder. Maybe you like paging through inspirational quotes by creative writers. Or maybe you enjoy going to the bookstore and picking up books that will teach you how to make the most of your own willpower. Find whatever triggers your positivity: Feeling good about your writing goals will get you far.

Make Staying Motivated Your Number One Priority!

If you have a good attitude, your submission strategy is more likely to succeed. Approach your hours spent making submissions by looking forward to them.

But if you find that researching and preparing your submissions get you down, and you really struggle with the process of making submissions due to time constraints or feelings of negativity, then it's probably best to find another way. Writer's Relief can research, prepare, and send your submissions out for you, depending on the strength of your writing and your needs.

It's rare that anything good comes out of negativity. So the most important thing that you can do to create a strong submission strategy is to find a way to feel positive and motivated about the work that you're doing—even if that means hiring someone else to do the work on your behalf. Better to feel good and channel all that good energy into your writing!

For more confidence-boosting tips, check out our book:

The Happy Writer:
Your Secret Weapon Against Rejection, Dejection,
Writer's Block, And The Emotional Pitfalls
Of The Writing Life.

If You Are Going To Hire A Submission Service...

Since we've mentioned our own services, we thought we should give you some pointers in case you choose to approach ANY submission service about getting help with sending out your work.

Resources and companies are available to you, but some of them are better than others. When deciding how to submit your work to literary journals or to agents, it's important to have a solid grasp of two key factors:

1. Know the lay of the land. Before you trust anyone else to make your submissions for you, or before you start making them yourself—know how the industry works. This way, you'll be more likely to pick up on anything that doesn't seem like a good practice. For example: Sending an agent more than one book proposal at once is generally a no-no.

2. Know your goals. Do you want to get your name out there by publishing in lit mags? Do you hope to connect with a literary agent who can represent your book? When you have a clear goal, you're more likely to attain it.

How To Find The Best Submission Help

Every writer is unique, and that means every writer has unique needs. When deciding if you want outside help in developing a submission strategy, ask yourself these three questions:

How much help with submissions do you want? Some writers just want a list of markets that are a good fit; they'll do the rest. Other writers want all-inclusive attention—they don't want to deal with any part of their submission strategy. Choosing this "complete coverage" route will maximize your time to write.

Write down your "best-case scenario" wish list for getting help with your submissions. What do you want someone else to do for you? Write your query letter? Track editors' responses to your poems? And so on.

Do you want expert support? If you're making submissions on your own, you'll need to have a reliable, tried-and-true support system of people you trust who are highly educated about the publishing industry and can advise you when questions arise.

Bonus Section

If you're going to use a submission assistance company, confirm that you'll have a knowledgeable professional on your team to help you navigate the inevitable bumps on the road to publishing.

What will you "pay" to reach your goals? No professional submission service is free. If you want someone to prepare your submissions or to conduct the research and give you names, you'll need to budget for the many hours a company must spend on these tasks.

If you go it alone, you'll have to "pay yourself" with your time spent researching—which means you'll not only have to find markets that work for you; you'll also need to eliminate hundreds or thousands that don't.

Weigh Your Options

Here are a few of the options available to you if you're looking for third-party assistance when making your writing submissions.

Hire an author submission service. If you're going to hire a company like Writer's Relief to help you, ask questions. Be sure you understand what you're getting into. And be wary of empty promises to make all your dreams come true or lengthy contracts that lock you in. Here are a few questions to ask:

- How do you research markets? Is research personalized?

- How many clients do you have? Any credible writers?

- What are your rates? Do you take commission?

- Who will be my contact at the company?

- Is any writer accepted or are there standards? What genres do you work with?

- Can I quit whenever I want?

- Are you acquiring any rights to my work?

Hire a personal assistant. We consider ourselves a team of personal assistants who have specialized knowledge about the publishing industry and work offsite (not in our clients' homes). You can hire a personal secretary to help you, but make sure it is someone with publishing experience.

Otherwise, you could waste as much time teaching someone how to make your submissions as if you did them yourself. Also, keep in mind that expertise matters when tough questions arise, and you may need to turn to professionals for answers.

DIY database websites and market books. If you're reading this book, you might have the right kind of self-starting attitude to orchestrate a successful submission strategy. Remember: You don't need anyone's help making submissions if you've got the focus, education, time, and drive to get it done!

Bonus Section

Free Resources On Our Website

Submit Write Now! Our weekly e-publication features interviews, news, strategies, tips, publishing leads, contests, and so much more!

Free Publishing Tool Kit. Our tool kits answer just about every question you have about how to develop a successful submission strategy. Visit our website to access Your Publishing Tool Kit: A Free Resource for Creative Writers. Here are some of our topics:

- How To Get Published: A Step-By-Step Guide For Beginning And Intermediate Writers
- Short Story Submissions: How To Submit Short Stories For Publication
- Poetry Submissions: How To Submit Your Poetry For Publication
- Literary Agent Submissions: How To Find Representation For Your Book Project
- Web Design: Online Marketing And Promotion Strategies For Writers
- Self-Publishing: Everything You Need To Know About Self-Publishing
- How To Handle Rejection: A Writer's Secret Weapon Against Rejection
- Staying Positive: Motivation, Encouragement, And Inspiration For Writers
- Writers Associations: Local And National Organizations For Writers

Informative YouTube videos. Quick, fun videos on all the writerly topics: favorite authors, just-for-fun facts, how-to info, grammar, and lots more.

Free consultation with a submission strategist. See if Writer's Relief has a plan that will work for your submissions to agents or lit mags.

PLUS—Are You Ready To Develop Your Web Presence? Sign up on www.WebDesignRelief.com to get your free report *The Writer's Essential Guide To Reputation-Building In A Digital World*—**the ultimate resource for building your online author platform** today! We are experts in designing websites specifically for authors. Check it out!

Having a website is an essential strategy; it's no longer optional for serious writers who want to make a name for themselves. We know what works for author websites.

Writer's Relief also offers social media support through our Virtual Assistant Program. Check out our marketing support options to help you boost your promotional efforts.

Are You Ready To Self-Publish? Sign up on www.SelfPublishingRelief.com to get your free guide *Uncovered: The 3 Best Book Cover Secrets* today! If you have exhausted traditional publishing options or just want to take charge from the start, this is the way to go, and Self-Publishing Relief will handle all the technical details. We offer a variety of packages and add-on options.

Final Thoughts

We understand that for some writers, the process of making submissions can be intimidating. And, frankly, that slightly nervous but excited feeling can result in a successful effort. So whether you're excited or anxious, embrace your feelings and forge ahead!

Remember, we're not saying there are strict rules about how to write a query letter. But if you're going to take your letter or strategy in a different direction than what we've recommended, we would simply advise you to do so with care. The etiquette of letter writing exists because it's functional for most writers and readers. You will find advice out there that differs from what we've written, but the process we've outlined for you is what we've found to be effective in our experience. And we've got a *LOT* of experience. We've been helping to match writers with agents and lit-mag editors since 1994.

- **Once your query letter is written, we can help you identify the best agents to query with your book.** Or, if you'd rather not write your own query, we can write it for you.

- **We can also target lit mags for submissions of poems, stories, essays, and book excerpts.** Targeting is 100 percent personalized. No submission spam, ever.

At Writer's Relief, we tackle as much of the submission process as you need, giving you more time to focus on what you love best: writing. We have built our business by genuinely caring about writers and the issues they face while trying to get published and succeed as authors.

Our clients have ranged from best sellers to promising unknowns. And there are many, many personally made video testimonials on our website that our clients voluntarily sent to us. You don't have to take *our* word for our expertise and effectiveness! You can also catch up with us on Facebook, Twitter, and many other social networks.

If you have questions we haven't answered in this book, write to us by visiting the contact form on our website.

We *know* you can do this. Stay strong. Be positive. Enjoy the process as a journey. Learn and grow.

We hope to hear from you—and we hope this book helped.

Sincerely,

Ronnie L. Smith

Ronnie L. Smith, President
Writer's Relief, Inc.
www.WritersRelief.com
(866) 405-3003

Other Books From Writer's Relief

The Happy Writer

Every writer suffers the writing blues at some point. And every *successful* writer finds a way through it. Intended for prose and poetry writers alike, *The Happy Writer* offers proven tips and motivational tools to overcome the practical and emotional issues you face as a writer.

Publishing Poetry & Prose in Literary Journals

You've written short stories, poetry, or essays, and you're ready to get published. What's next? Now you need an effective, long-term submission strategy that gets results. *Publishing Poetry & Prose in Literary Journals* explains everything you need to know—and do—to get your writing published.

The Writer's Relief Field Guide To Literary Agents

Whether you're a new writer or a veteran author, finding a literary agent is the best hope for getting your book published. But, as any writer with a book project will tell you, capturing the attention and interest of a literary agent is easier said than done. You need a guide.

More information is available on our website store at www.WritersRelief.com.

Made in United States
Orlando, FL
30 July 2023